130 NEW WINEMAKING RECIPES

C. J. J. BERRY

An Amateur Winemaker Book

Special Interest Model Books Ltd.
P.O. Box 327
Poole
Dorset
BH15 2RG
England
www.specialinterestmodelbooks.co.uk

First published by Argus Books Ltd, 1985
Third edition
Reprinted 1981, 1982, 1983, 1984, 1985, 1988, 1991, 1992, 1993, 1995, 1997

This edition published by Special Interest Model Books Ltd. 2002

Reprinted 2003, 2005

ISBN 1-90084-163-X

Printed and bound in Great Britain by Biddles Ltd, King's Lynn, Norfolk

Introducing this book . . .

First published in 1963 to augment the recipes in "First Steps in Winemaking", by the same author, "130 New Winemaking Recipes" has proved an enormous success in its own right, running through two editions. Twenty-three impressions of the second edition have been printed, bringing the total sale to date to over 500,000 copies.

In this third edition, produced in the popular A5 format, the opportunity has been taken to up-date the general winemaking information and to adjust all the recipes to modern requirements. Quantities are now in metric measures, but the old Imperial measures are still given as well, for the convenience of readers who prefer "the old ways", but please note that quantities are not exactly equivalent but are rounded up or down to give convenient amounts in either scale. Almost all recipes make exactly one gallon of wine and not "one gallon plus".

The book contains over 130 tried, reliable recipes, many of which are my own, and many of which were originally compiled by Mr C. Shave, the well-known Birmingham winemaker, Mr Bryan Acton, Mr Peter Duncan, Mr Humfrey Wakefield, and other winemaking friends. The cartoons are by Rex Royle, the well-known winemaking cartoonist.

Whilst in the main the recipes are supplementary to the 130 or so which appear in "First Steps in Winemaking", we have taken care also to include certain well-tried favourites which have stood the test of time, and the book is therefore self-contained. The two books together present a unique collection of reliable recipes. We particularly recommend the peach recipe and the "variations upon a theme" when using bananas, elderberries or rosehips.

"130 New Winemaking Recipes" will enable you to start making country wines successfully, with the minimum of theory. We hope that you enjoy it, and that many new and exciting wines will grace your cellar as a result of it.

Andover 1981

WELCOME TO WINEMAKING!

Nowadays there is a great book in winemaking, and thousands of people are discovering for themselves the truth of what I have been propounding for the last 40 years, that winemaking is a really exciting and absorbing hobby, with an enjoyable "end product", to use the TV idiom.

Winemaking shops have made their appearance in most towns, and attractively packed winemaking kits can be bought in them and in many chain stores. There is certainly no difficulty nowadays about finding a source of supply.

Many winemakers, however, want to take their winemaking beyond the making up of a simple kit according to the manufacturer's instructions – "winemaking by numbers". They want to be able to make their own wines from fruit or other ingredients garnered from their garden or from the hedgerows. It's more fun, and it's certainly a whole lot cheaper!

Legally, the position is that you may make as much wine or beer as you like at home – and some enthusiasts make hundreds of gallons a year – *but not a drop of it must be sold, or distilled,* and separating the alcohol by deep freezing is equally illegal.

Making wine at home is *not* difficult, despite what some of the experts say. Most of the utensils can be found in any kitchen – a large saucepan or kettle for boiling (stainless steel, aluminium, or sound enamel ware, but not iron, brass or copper), a 6 litre (1½ gallon) or 9 litre (2 gallon) white polythene bucket, a 25 litre (5 gallon) white plastic fermenting bin, bottles and corks, and a stainless steel or polypropylene spoon.

Other items which will be found useful are glass 1-gallon jars (the sort with ear handles), fermentation traps, to keep the wine from contamination, a yard of acrylic tubing for siphoning, a corking tool, a large plastic funnel for filtering (the larger the better) and, if you wish to go further into the "mysteries", a hydrometer to help calculate the strength of your wines. This is dealt with in detail in *First Steps in Winemaking.*

Notice that your utensils, apart from the boiler and crock already mentioned, should be of glass, non-resinous wood (oak, ash or beech), or high-density white plastic.

CLEANLINESS

Everything must be kept scrupulously clean by the use of boiling water or by the use of cleaning and sterilising solutions on bottles and apparatus.

Cleaning solutions:

Soda: 125g (4oz) washing soda in 5 litres (1 gallon) water.

Hypochlorite: 25g (1fl oz) domestic bleach in 5 litres (1 gallon) water.

Rinse well afterwards in cold water in both cases.

Sterilising solution:

6 Campden tablets and 20g ($\frac{1}{2}$oz) citric acid in 1 pint water. Avoid inhaling. Rinse well afterwards.

Chempro is a marvellous proprietary cleaner/steriliser used at 1 dessertspoon per gallon.

WHAT WINE IS

Any wine initially consists of: 1, flavouring; 2, water; 3, sugar; 4, acid; 5, tannin, and 6, yeast and nutrient. Another ingredient, which is perhaps the hardest to find, is time!

All that happens when yeast, a living organism, is put into a sugary solution, is that it feeds upon the sugar, converting it roughly half to alcohol and half to carbon dioxide, by weight, so that one finishes up with a pleasantly-flavoured alcoholic drink.

We extract the flavour from fruits and vegetables by boiling them, by soaking them in cold water, or by a combination of the two (ie pouring boiling water on them and leaving them to soak). Or we can simply express the juice by means of a press or juice extractor, and add the required amount of water to it.

An even simpler way is to buy some pectin-destroying enzyme such as Pectinol, Pektolase, or Rohament P, and add small quantities of this to the chopped-up fruit as directed. It will break down the fruit tissues and release the juice, which can then be strained off. It is a good idea to use this in most fruit wines.

As regards sugar, one need only remember that 1 kg (2lb 3oz) *in* the gallon will produce a dry wine of table strength. 1.25 kg (2$\frac{1}{2}$lb) will produce a medium, stronger wine, and that sugar beyond that, and certainly beyond 1.360 kg (3lb) will merely serve to make the wine sweeter, since it will not be converted to alcohol. Such sweetening sugar is better added in 100g (4oz) doses towards the end of the fermentation.

Note that there is a difference between *in* the gallon and *to* the gallon. "In the gallon" means that you have to have so much sugar and make the total volume up to 1 gallon. "To the gallon" means that you add your sugar to 1 gallon of water, and therefore finish up with more than 1 gallon. And, of course, you need more sugar (and ingredients) to achieve the same strength.

YEAST

There are many types of yeast. We would recommend either a good-quality wine yeast, liquid or granulated, obtainable from any winemaking shop. Sometimes however, beginners like to use a bakers or brewers yeast because it gives a more frothy, and therefore comforting ferment, but the wine produced is not of such good quality. All will make wine, of varying quality, and usually the decision as to which type to use resolves itself into a matter of personal preference.

IN ALL THE FOLLOWING RECIPES USE A WINE YEAST OR 1 LEVEL TEASPOONFUL OF A GOOD GRANULATED YEAST. WITH WINE YEASTS FULL INSTRUCTIONS ARE SUPPLIED.

Beware of "No yeast" recipes. No liquor will work *without* yeast; it means that you are relying upon the natural yeast in the fruit, or, if you have killed that by the use of boiling water or sulphite, on any "wild" yeast which happens to be in the air . . . and the gamble may not come off.

NUTRIENT

Yeast nutrient can be used to "boost" the action of the yeast and is particularly recommended in flower, mead and other wines where the liquor is likely to be deficient in certain trace minerals. One can obtain nutrient ready made up, but why not make up your own, from these chemicals (which you can buy, quite cheaply, from any winemaking shop or chemist)?

For 1 gallon:
$\frac{1}{2}$ teaspoon ammonium phosphate
$\frac{1}{2}$ teaspoon ammonium sulphate
1 3mg Vitamin B_1 tablet

6

ACID AND TANNIN

An important constituent of wine is acid, which can be included in the form of citric, tartaric, or malic acid. Citric acid is the most popular and, if you are formulating a recipe, include at least one level teaspoon with fruit wines and as much as four when using non-acid ingredients such as flowers or grain.

The inclusion of some tannin will make a marked improvement in many wines, giving them that desirable "bite" without which they can be "flabby" and uninteresting. Buy it at your wine shop and use only sparingly, as directed.

FERMENTATION

The fermentation should be in two stages–the first vigorous one when the yeast is multiplying itself to the required level, and needs air for the process. For this it is advisable to have your jar only three-quarters full, to allow room for frothing. For the secondary, quieter one, the jar is topped up with water and the air excluded, an unkind device which forces the yeast to produce more alcohol! That is why one should employ the modern device of a fermentation lock at this stage.

This will act as a barrier to infection, and to the vinegar bacteria and other bugs which are the winemaker's biggest enemies.

WINEMAKING SUMMARISED

1. Extract flavour from ingredients by pressing, boiling or soaking in bowl or polythene bucket.
2. Add sugar and yeast and ferment for up to 10 days in a polythene bucket or bin in a warm place 20-25°C (70-75°F).
3. Strain off, put into fermentation bottle, and fit fermentation trap, filling to within an inch of bottom of cork. Temperature: about 15°C (60°F). This fermentation will be much softer and will proceed for some weeks, but eventually all bubbling will cease.
4. "Rack", i.e. siphon, the cleared wine off the "lees", or yeast deposit at the bottom of the jar. This should be repeated about a month later, and usually a third racking after a further three weeks is beneficial. By now the temperature should have been reduced to 15°C (60°F) and the wine should be quite stable, with no risk of explosions!
5. Bottle when wine is about six months old and cork securely. Bottles are then stored, on their sides preferably, in a room at about 13°C (55°F).

DO'S AND DON'TS

Do ...

Keep things very clean.

Keep air away except during first few days, and even then keep brew closely covered.

Use fermentation trap for secondary fermentation.

Keep fermenting bottles full to within one inch of bottom of cork.

Strain wine well initially or the wine will be hard to clarify.

Keep a book and jot down all you do, so that you can repeat it.

Use new corks.

Keep red wines in dark bottles, to preserve their colour.

Don't ...

Allow infection to get at brew.

Forget to stir the "must" twice daily.

Ferment in a metal vessel.

Put wine in old, damp bottles, or it may be infected.

Let sediment lie at bottom of jar or it will impart a bad taste to the wine.

Rush a wine: give it time!

Use finings or filter unnecessarily; most wines will clear of their own accord, given time.

Use too much sugar, or your wines will be oversweet.

ALMOND (Calcavella) WINE

By Mrs Maie Davis, of 4 Hampton Court, King's Lynn
Ingredients:

450g	**(1lb)**	**raisins**
		3 lemons
1kg	**(2¼lb)**	**granulated sugar**
55g	**(2oz)**	**almonds** (sweet, a few bitter may be added)
		Yeast and nutrient (she uses a Sauternes)
Water to 4.5 litres (1 gallon)		

Method:

Chop the almonds and raisins and put them in muslin with the rind of the lemons. Boil gently in 3 litres (5½ pints) water. Add the sugar, stirring to dissolve, and the juice of lemons. Cool to blood heat and add yeast. Ferment 3-4 days, then strain into gallon jar to ferment, top up to bottom of neck with cold water, and fit trap.

APPLE WINE

Apples make a truly delicious table wine, in the making of which there are only two difficulties– the pulping and the pressing. Cutting up large quantities of apples with a knife is a tedious and blister-making business and ideally the problem is solved by means of one of the neat apple mills or juice extractors that can now be obtained. Failing this, however, the job can be almost equally comfortably tackled with a chopping board and a small kindling chopper, holding it near the head and allowing the weight of the blade to do all the work. *Much* easier than a knife; the ancient Chinese knew a thing or two when they used heavy kitchen implements for chopping up food! A press for the pulp is a great help, but if you cannot buy, beg, or borrow one wrap your apple pulp in stout cloths, place the "pudding" on a strong open framework or laths (an iron footscraper or sieve) over a large vessel, and press upon it with your weight with your fists, and this will extract most of the juice.

An even easier method is to break down the fruit with an anti-pectin enzyme and then strain it through close-mesh nylon material.

The apples you use are important. The best eating apples do not make the best wine; usually the "rougher" the apple the better the result. Cider apples are ideal, cookers are a good second-best, and 1lb of crab apples in 10 will result in a great improvement. Russets are to be avoided, and a good plan is to use as big a mixture of types as possible.

If you have a real glut of apples use as much as 10kg (24lb) to $4\frac{1}{2}$ litres (1 gallon) of water (the water will not cover them during mashing) and you will get a truly glorious wine; if you have fewer, use 5kg (12lb) to the gallon and you will still get a delicious, but less full-bodied wine. The quantity can even be cut down to 2.5kg (6lb) but the general opinion is that then the flavour and body are not wholly satisfactory.

Ingredients:

5-10kg (12-24lb)	**mixed apples**
1.3kg (3lb)	**white sugar to 4.5 litres (1 gallon) of liquor**
4.5 litres (1 gallon)	**water**
	Yeast and nutrient
	Pectic enzyme

Method:

Chop or crush the apples into small pieces, put into a polythene bucket or dustbin, and add the water (cold) the pectic enzyme, and two level teaspoons of a granulated yeast. Leave for about a week, closely covered, stirring vigorously from the bottom at least twice a day to bring the lower apple to the top. This system breaks all the accepted rules in that the fruit is not sterilised, either with boiling water, or with sulphite, yet we have never known the recipe to fail. Keep the bucket in a fairly warm place, of course. Then strain the juice from the pulp. Press the pulp as efficiently as you can and add the juice to the rest of the liquor. Measure, and for every gallon add 2.5kg (3lb) of sugar. Put into cask or other fermenting vessel and fit fermentation lock, racking when it has cleared. The wine will probably be ready for drinking within six months, but is vastly improved by being matured in wood for a year. A further improvement can be effected by using a Sauternes yeast. If a really dry wine is required reduce the sugar by 225g ($\frac{1}{2}$lb).

APRICOT AND DATE

(See under Date and Apricot)

APRICOT SHERRY

Ingredients:

500g	(1lb)	dried apricots
1.3kg	(3lb)	sugar
		1 cup strong tea
3 litres	(6 pints)	water
		Sherry yeast
		Yeast nutrient
		Pectic enzyme

Method:

Wash the apricots well, and slice. Add 3 litres of water and simmer for 30 minutes. Do not boil. Strain, add the sugar and boil for a further five minutes. Add a breakfast cupful of strong tea and pour all into a gallon jar. When cool add the pectic enzyme. Twenty-four hours later add the sherry culture or a level teaspoon of dried yeast, fit a fermentation lock in the neck of the jar, which should only be nine-tenths full, and set aside to ferment.

After a month empty the liquid from the fermentation lock, but lightly plug its upper end with cotton wool, and replace it, in order to give the sherry yeast the air it needs (if "ordinary" yeast is being used this is unnecessary).

Leave undisturbed for at least six months, then rack off into a clean jar, together with a little of the cleanest yeast from the bottom of the vessel and bring into a warm room for a few days to speed the final fermentation. Top up with cold water if necessary to bottom of neck. When the fermentation has picked up remove vessel to a cool spot and leave for a further six months before bottling. When a year old, it is a most satisfactory sherry-flavoured wine.

BANANA WINE

Ingredients:

1.3kg	(3lb)	Peeled bananas
225g	($\frac{1}{2}$lb)	banana skins
100g	($\frac{1}{4}$lb)	raisins
1kg	(2lb)	sugar
		Yeast and nutrient
		Pectic enzyme
		1 lemon, 1 orange

Water to: 4.5 litres (1 gallon)

Method:

Use black or spotted bananas, whatever you can scrounge. Place bananas and fruit peel into a cloth bag and put the bag, tied up, into a large saucepan or boiler with 3 litres (5 pints, 5oz) water. Bring to the boil, then gently simmer for half an hour. Pour the hot liquor over the sugar and fruit juice, and when the cloth bag has cooled squeeze it with the hands to extract as much liquor as possible. When all the liquor is lukewarm 20°C (70°F) add the yeast, pectic enzyme and nutrient. Leave it in a warm place for a week, stirring daily, then pour into a glass jar and move it to a cooler place; it will be a thick-looking mess, like a lot of soapsuds. Keep it well covered and in a couple of months it will have a large sediment at the bottom. Siphon off, then add the chopped raisins. Top up to bottom of neck with cold water if necessary. Fit an air lock and siphon off again after four months; by then it will have started to clear. Leave a further six months before sampling. It improves the longer you keep it.

"Yes, you can make wine from almost ANYthing . . ."

12

SPICED BANANA WINE

Ingredients:

1.5kg	(3lb)	bananas (including skins) or 6oz dried variety
30g	(1oz)	cloves
30g	(1oz)	ginger
1.25kg	(2½lb)	sugar
15g	(½oz)	citric acid (or 3 lemons, no pith, in lieu)
500ml	(1½ pints)	strong tea (a teaspoonful of grape tannin)
3.5 litres	(6 pints)	water
		Yeast nutrient and activated wine yeast

Method:

Thinly slice the bananas and skins. Place these into the initial fermentation bin or bucket together with sugar, cloves and ginger, and pour in boiling water. Stir to dissolve the sugar and when cool add the citric acid and strong tea. Introduce the activated wine yeast and nutrient. Ferment on the fruit for 10 days, then strain into fermentation jar. Fit airlock and ferment to a finish in the normal way, racking as necessary in due course.

DRIED BANANAS

Ingredients:

335g	(12oz)	dried bananas
225g	(8oz)	raisins
		Two level teaspoons citric acid
1kg	(2lb 3oz)	sugar
		Pectic enzyme
		1 sherry yeast (liquid or dry)
Water to 4.5 litres (1 gallon)		

Method:

Simmer the dried bananas in the pressure cooker for 10 minutes, then put into fermenting bucket and make up to 3 litres (7 pints) with cold water. Add the raisins, citric acid and sugar. When quite cool add the pectin destroying enzyme and, 24 hours later, the yeast. Ferment on the pulp for seven days, stirring every day and keeping closely covered.

Strain into a gallon jar, make up to 1 gallon with a little cold water and ferment under the protection of a fermentation lock in the usual manner.

BANANA AND DRIED ELDERBERRY

Ingredients:

900g	**(2lb)**	**bananas (including skins) or 100g (4oz) dried variety**
500g	**(1lb)**	**dried elderberries**
1.3kg	**(3lb)**	**sugar**
15g	**(½oz)**	**citric acid (or 3 lemons, no pith, in lieu)**
		A pinch of grape tannin
3.5 litres (6 pints)		**water**
		Yeast nutrient and wine yeast

Method:

Slice up thinly the bananas, including skins, and place in the initial fermentation bucket, together with the dried elderberries and sugar. Pour in boiling water and stir until sugar is dissolved. When cool add the citric acid and tannin. Introduce the yeast nutrient and activated wine yeast and leave to ferment on the fruit for 10 days, then siphon into fermentation jar and top up to bottom of neck if necessary. Fit airlock, and leave to ferment in normal way, racking as necessary in due course.

BANANA AND FIG WINE

Ingredients:

900g	(2lb)	bananas (including skins) or 100g (4oz) dried variety
1kg	(2lb)	dried figs
1.3kg	(3lb)	sugar
15g	($\frac{1}{2}$oz)	citric acid (or 3 lemons, no pith, in lieu)
		A pinch of grape tannin
3 litres	(6 pints)	water
		Yeast nutrient and activated wine yeast
		Pectic enzyme

Method:

Chop the bananas and skins into small thin pieces. Similarly chop the dried figs and place these together with the sugar into a polythene bucket or bin. Pour the boiling water over the chopped fruit and then stir well. When cool add citric acid, tannin, and pectic enzyme, 24 hours later introduce the yeast nutrient and activated wine yeast. Ferment on the pulp for 10 days, closely covered, then strain into fermentation jar. Top up with a little cold water if necessary. Fit airlock and allow to ferment in normal way. Rack as necessary in due course.

BANANA AND PARSNIP WINE

Ingredients:

900g	(2lb)	bananas (including skins) or 100g (4oz) dried variety
2kg	(5lb)	parsnips
1.3kg	(3lb)	sugar
15g	($\frac{1}{2}$oz)	citric acid or (3 lemons, no pith, in lieu)
		A pinch of grape tannin
3 litres	(6 pints)	water
		Yeast nutrient and activated wine yeast
		Pectic enzyme

Method:

Scrub and thinly slice parsnips and boil slowly until tender, then pour the extract over the chopped bananas and skins. Add the sugar and stir until dissolved. When cool add the citric acid, tannin and pectic enzyme. 24 hours later introduce the activated wine yeast and nutrient and ferment on the banana pulp for 10 days. Strain into fermentation jar and top up to bottom of neck if neccessary with cold water. Fit airlock and allow to ferment in the normal way, racking into clean jar when it clears.

BANANA AND PRUNE WINE

Ingredients:

900g	(2lb)	bananas (including skins) or 100g (4oz) dried variety
1kg	(2lb)	sugar
1kg	(2lb)	prunes
225g	($\frac{1}{2}$lb)	raisins
20g	($\frac{1}{2}$oz)	citric acid or (3 lemons, not pith, in lieu)
		A pinch of grape tannin
3.5 litres (6 pints)		water
		Pectic enzyme
		Yeast nutrient and activated wine yeast

Method:

Thinly slice the bananas and skins, also slice in half the prunes. Place into the initial fermentation bucket, add the chopped raisins and sugar. Pour in the boiling water and stir until sugar is dissolved. When cool add the citric acid, tannin and pectic enzyme. Next day introduce the yeast nutrient and activated wine yeast. Ferment on the pulp for 10 days, then strain into fermentation jar and top up with cold water. Fit air lock and leave to ferment in normal way, racking as necessary in due course.

BANANA AND RICE

Ingredients:

900g	(2lb)	bananas (including skins) or 100g (4oz) dried variety
1.3kg	(3lb)	paddy rice (with husk)
225g	($\frac{1}{2}$lb)	stoned raisins
1.3kg	(3lb)	sugar
20g	($\frac{1}{2}$oz)	citric acid (or 3 lemons, no pith, in lieu)
		A pinch of grape tannin
4 litres	(7 pints)	water
		Yeast and nutrient
		Pectic enzyme

16

Method:

Place the finely chopped bananas and skins, paddy rice and stoned raisins, together with the sugar, into your polythene bin or bucket. Pour in the boiling water and stir until sugar is dissolved. When cool add the citric acid, tannin and enzyme. Next day introduce the yeast nutrient and activated wine yeast and ferment for 10 days on the pulp. Then strain into fermentation jar. Top up the jar with cold water if necessary, fit airlock and ferment to completion in the normal way, racking as necessary in due course.

BANANA AND ROSE HIP SHELL WINE

Ingredients:

1kg	(2lb)	bananas (including skins) or 100g (4oz) dried variety
225g	(½lb)	dried rose hips 100g (4oz) rose hip shells (A handful of Hawthorn berries or (some) dried Elderberries will give this wine an excellent colour)
1.3kg	(3lb)	sugar
15g	(½oz)	citric acid
		A pinch of grape tannin
4 litres	(7 pints)	water
		Yeast nutrient and activated wine yeast
		Pectic enzyme

Method:

Chop into thin slices the bananas and skins and pour over boiling water. Add sugar and stir until dissolved. The rose hips, hawthorn berries and elderberries, indeed all three if desired, should then be added. When cool add citric acid, tannin, and pectic enzyme. Twenty-four hours later introduce the yeast nutrient and activated wine yeast and ferment for 10 days on the pulp. Then strain into fermentation jar and top up with cold water. Fit air lock and ferment in the normal way, racking as necessary in due course.

DRIED BANANA AND ROSE HIP

Ingredients:

100g	(4oz)	rose hip shells
350g	(12oz)	dried bananas
		Pectic enzyme
		2 teaspoons citric acid
1kg	(2lb 3oz)	sugar
		A Tokaier yeast and nutrient

Water to: 4½ litres (1 gallon)

Method:

Bring 2 litres of water to the boil and pour over the rosehip shells. Simmer the dried bananas in another 2 litres water in the pressure cooker for 10 minutes. Mix the two lots, and add the citric acid and sugar. Stir well. When cool, about 20°C (70°F) add the pectic enzyme and a few hours later the yeast and nutrient. Ferment on the pulp for seven days, stirring every day. Strain off into a gallon jar, top up with water, fit air lock and ferment under a fermentation lock until clear, in the usual manner. Then siphon into a clean jar. Leave for a further three months before bottling.

BANANA AND SARSAPARILLA

Ingredients:

1.5kg	(3lb)	bananas (including skins) or 6oz dried variety
55g	(2oz)	Sarsaparilla
1.25 kg	(2lb 11oz)	sugar
15g	($\frac{1}{2}$oz)	citric acid (or 3 lemons, no pith, in lieu)
		A teaspoonful grape tannin
4 litres	7 pints	water
		Yeast nutrient and activated wine yeast

"... and now may I introduce your Chairman ..."

19

Method:

Thinly slice the bananas and skins and place in the initial fermentation vessel. Add the sugar and pour in boiling water. Stir to dissolve, then add the Sarsaparilla. When cool, add the citric acid and tannin. Introduce the yeast nutrient and activated wine yeast. Ferment on the pulp for 10 days, then strain into fermention jar and top up with cold water. Fit air lock and ferment to a finish in the normal way, racking as necessary in due course.

BARLEY

(and other grain wines)

Once the main rush of the winemaking season is over, why not make a good stock of cereal wine? The usual favourites are barley, wheat or maize, although some like rice, and they can all be made from the same basic recipe, using 1lb of grain. Barley gives the smoothest wine, with most body, maize is intermediate in this respect, and wheat wine tends to be thinner and have more bite, and is often said to have a slight whisky flavour (although not, of course, whisky strength).

Ingredients:

450g	**(1lb)**	**barley, maize or wheat**
1.25kg	**(2lb 8oz)**	**white sugar**
450g	**(1lb)**	**raisins**
		2 lemons, 1 orange
		Yeast nutrient

Water to: 4.5 litre (1 gallon)

Method:

Wash the grain, then soak it overnight in 500ml (1 pint) of the water. The next day mince both grain and raisins in a domestic mincer (using the coarsest holes) and put into a crock or bowl with the sugar and the thinly-pared rinds of the fruit. Pour over them 4 litres (7 pints) of water, boiling. Cover. Cool to 20°C, (70°F) (tepid), then add the juice of the lemons and orange, the yeast and yeast nutrient. Cover closely and leave in a warm place 17-20°C (65-70°F). for a week, stirring daily. Then strain into a fermenting jar, topping up with cold water if necessary, and fit air lock; siphon off the lees when it clears, and refit lock. Leave for a further three months or so before racking into clean bottles.

When making rice wine use the above recipe, but use 1.3kg (3lb) of rice instead of 450g.

BEERS AND STOUTS

MORGAN'S ALE

Ingredients:

500g	**(1lb)**	**malt extract**
225g	**(½lb)**	**sugar**
30g	**(1oz)**	**hops (or to taste)**
4.5 litres	**(1 gallon)**	**water**
		Yeast

Method:

Boil up the ingredients in 2 litres (½ gallon) of water in pressure cooker for 30 minutes. Strain, add 2 litres (½ gallon) of cold water, and yeast. Set aside to ferment, closely covered, and skim off the "cap" every 24 hours. When fermentation has apparently ceased (usually about a week), bottle in 1 litre (quart) beer bottles, adding a level teaspoon of sugar to each bottle. Cork tightly and seal with crown caps or screw stoppers. Stand in a cool place to clear. The beer is usually ready to drink after another fortnight.

"... he does an awful lot of wine judging ..."

BERRYBREW
(a strong bitter)

Ingredients:

1.8kg	(4lb)	malt extract
1.8kg	(4lb)	sugar
100g	(4oz)	hops
		10ml (1 dessertspoon) Crosse and Blackwell's gravy browning
		1 level teaspoon citric acid
		2 teaspoons salt
20 litres	(4½ gallons)	water
		Yeast

Method:

Put hops (if preferred in muslin bag), salt and gravy browning (which is only caramel colouring) into some or all of the water. (I use 10 litres), but make sure you have a few extra hops to add later. Bring to the boil. Simmer for 40 minutes.

Add a few loose hops, simmer for a further five minutes.

Meanwhile stand the jars of malt extract in hot water for 10 minutes to facilitate pouring; then put the malt extract and sugar into a polythene bin and strain the hopped wort on to them. Stir well to dissolve, and add the acid. Make up to the desired quantity with the remainder of the water (2-3 gallons) cold. (If using a carboy for fermentation the whole of the wort thus prepared can be poured into it when cool.)

Allow to cool to 20°C (70°F) and then add a good brewer's yeast and nutrient. Use proprietary yeasts in quantities recommended, with granulated yeast, use 3 *level* teaspoons. Close the bin with a polythene sheet secured with elastic (or, if carboy, with air lock). Fermentation should be vigorous in 36 hours, complete in 10 days.

When the surface of the beer has cleared, and only tiny bubbles are visible in a ring in the centre (the gravity *must* be 1010 or below, and preferably down to 1000-1002), bottle in strong 1-quart beer or cider flagons. Fill to within 1½ inches of bottom of stopper, add *one level teaspoon* of white sugar to each bottle (not more!) and screw down hard. Put the beer in a cool (not cold) place and it will be clear and ready for drinking after a fortnight or so.

BOYS' BITTER

Ingredients:

450g	**(1lb)**	**malt extract**
30g	**(1oz)**	**hops**
4.5 litres	**(1 gallon)**	**water**
		Yeast

Method:

This is an excellent basic beer, and its bitterness can be adjusted by increasing or decreasing the amount of hops proportionately. Since it is ready to drink after just over a week, you can experiment with two or three consecutive gallons and get the flavour to your personal taste before multiplying the quantities to make the beer in bulk. Whilst experimenting, pay regard principally to flavour, rather than to clarity, for to obtain complete clarity it is necessary to store the beer in a cool place for a month.

Bring the water to the boil, add the malt extract and hops, and simmer for an hour and a half. "Top up" to the original volume with more water, then strain through muslin or close-mesh flour sieve into a large fermenting bin or vessel. (If you use normal one-gallon

"That last lot of beer seems extra gassy!"

23

fermentation jars they must not be filled beyond the shoulder, because of the froth, so use several.)

Add your yeast, and keep in a warm place 20°C (70°F) for four days. Then siphon the beer off the yeast deposit into strong bottles. Add a cube of sugar to each bottle, and tie down the cork. (It is best not to use screw stoppers until you have really mastered the art of brewing; a tied-down cork will always give warning of impending disaster; a screw-stopper will not!) Move the beer into a cool place; it will be drinkable in another week.

OATMEAL STOUT

Ingredients:

350g	(¾lb)	rye
225g	(½lb)	black malt
225g	(½lb)	pale malt
150g	(6oz)	oatmeal
60g	(2oz)	hops
1.8kg	(4lb)	sugar
18 litres	(4 gallons)	water

Method:

Crack the pale malt (but not the black) with a rolling pin and put all the malt into about 8 litres (two gallons) of water at 60°C (150°F) in a two-gallon bucket. Then insert a 50-watt glass immersion heater (costing about £1, such as is used in tropical fish tanks), wrap the bucket in a blanket or thick cloth, and leave the heater switched on for a period of eight hours; this can conveniently be done overnight. This will maintain the brew at the ideal temperature for mashing (65°C or 150°F) and extraction will be first-rate. Then pour into a boiler and add the hops, rye and oatmeal, and boil for an hour, adding a few extra hops in the last five minutes. Strain into the fermenting vessel on to the sugar and make up to just over four gallons with cold water. Cool to 25°C (75°F) before adding the yeast and fermenting in the usual way. When the surface of the wort begins to clear and bubbles are collecting centrally (or when the S.G. is nearing 1001) bottle, adding one level teaspoon of sugar to each quart beer bottle. Store in a cool, dark place until the homebrew clears, and pour out carefully and steadily to avoid disturbing sediment.

If you cannot obtain an immersion heater to do the extraction properly, all the ingredients (except, of course, the yeast) can be simmered in all, or some, of the water, the sugar added, and the wort then fermented, but the resultant "stout" will not be of quite such high quality.

SEWARD ALE
(to make 5 gallons)

Ingredients:

22 litres	**(5 gallons)**	water
		Yeast
675g	**(1½lb)**	brown sugar
45g	**(1½oz)**	crushed barley
900g	**(1lb)**	brown malt extract
85g	**(3oz)**	hops

"And these are two I keep for my personal use."

25

Method:

Soak the barley in a little water overnight and run it through a mincer. Boil the hops (the packeted variety will do), malt (obtainable from most *Amateur Winemaker* advertisers or from the chemist) and barley for 30 minutes, in 9 litres (two gallons) of the water. Strain on to the sugar and stir to dissolve it, then add the remaining water (cold). Allow to cool to about 20°C (70°F) then add yeast, a good beer yeast or a level teaspoon of granulated yeast. Cover closely and allow to ferment in a warm place for 48 hours, skimming frequently. By then the S.G. should have dropped to about 1010. Bottle without disturbing the sediment, by using a siphon tube. Keep the beer another five or six days in a cool place, after which it can be drunk, but it will be vastly improved for being left another three weeks. If a darker beer is required (this one is light in colour) add up to 15g ($\frac{1}{2}$oz) liquorice to the five gallons.

Can't think where that judge has got to.

BEETROOT WINE

Ingredients:

1.8kg	(4lb)	young beetroot
1.2kg	(2½lb)	sugar
		Yeast and nutrient
		1 lemon
		4 to 6 cloves
		½oz root ginger

Water to: 4.5 litres (1 gallon)

This recipe uses young beetroot, and the secret is to make sure that they are not overboiled.

Method:

Wash the beetroot thoroughly, then slice thinly. Bring to the boil in 3.5 litres (6 pints) of water, with the thinly peeled rind of the lemon, the cloves and the ginger. Simmer until the beetroot is tender and loses its colour. Strain on to the sugar preferably in a polythene bucket. Stir well to dissolve and when lukewarm, 20°C (70°F) add the juice of the lemon and the yeast (a pre-prepared wine yeast, or a level teaspoonful of granulated yeast). Cover and leave in a warm place, 17-20°C (65-70°F) for two days to begin fermentation. Then pour into fermenting vessel, topping up with cold water, and fit fermentation trap. Siphon off when it clears, and bottle when stable in dark bottles to preserve its colour.

BEETROOT AND PARSNIP WINE

(by C. Shave)

Ingredients:

1kg	(2lb)	frosted parsnips
1kg	(2lb)	old beetroot
1.2kg	(2½lb)	sugar
		Grape tannin
		Pectic enzyme
		2 lemons
		2 oranges or ½oz citric acid
		Yeast nutrient
		Yeast (selected wine or general purpose)

Water to: 4.5 litres (1 gallon)

Method:

Wash the roots well (do not peel), slice thinly and place in 3.5 litres (6 pints) of water with the grated peel (no white pith) of the fruit, and the tea. Simmer until the roots are tender. (N.B.—Any overboiling may result in a cloudy wine). Strain and dissolve the sugar in the liquor. When cool add the pectic enzyme and 24 hours later the yeast; thereafter continue as for beetroot wine.

BEET AND PINEAPPLE WINE

. . . an unusual combination, but, having tasted it, we can vouch for the fact that it makes an excellent wine. The recipe is that of Mrs M. Paton, of Muirend, Stewarton, Kilmarnock, Ayrshire.

Ingredients:

1.8kg	(4lb)	beet
500g	(1lb)	raisins
1kg	(2lb 3oz)	sugar
		1 large or 2 small pineapples
		2 lemons
Water to: 4.5 litres (1 gallon)		
		Yeast

Method:

Wash the beet, but do not peel them, and cut into small pieces. Peel pineapples thickly. Put peel of pineapples and cut-up beet into pan, cover with 3.5 litres of water, and boil till beet is tender, but not mushy. (The remainder of the pineapples can be eaten). Put sugar, raisins (washed and chopped) and sliced lemons into bucket, and strain the hot liquor over them, stirring to dissolve the sugar. Allow to cool to 70°F, then add the yeast (and, preferably, some nutrient for it), cover with a thick cloth, and stand in a warm place to ferment. After five days or so, strain into fermenting jar, top up to bottom of neck with cold water, and fit trap. Rack off and bottle when wine has completely cleared. If after a while it throws a sediment, rack again. As an alternative, use 1.3kg (3lb) beet and 450g (1lb) black grapes. Crush the grapes and add them to the sugar, raisins, etc, in the bucket. Use dark bottles.

BILBERRY (See Elderberry, p. 56)

BILBERRY DRIED (See Elderberry, p. 56)

BLACKBERRY WINE (1)

Ingredients:

1.3kg	**(3lb)**	**blackberries**
1.25kg	**(2lb 11oz)**	**sugar**
		Yeast and nutrient
4 litres	**(7 pints)**	**water**

Method:

Pick the blackberries when they are fully ripe, and use only those of the best quality. Crush them in a plastic bucket with a stainless steel or wooden spoon and add water, mixing thoroughly. Allow them to stand overnight, then strain them through a nylon sieve on to the sugar, and stir well to dissolve. Add yeast and nutrient, cover closely with a sheet of polythene or thick cloth, and leave in a warm place 20-25°C (70-75°F) for a week; then, when the first vigorous ferment has subsided, stir, and transfer to fermenting jar. Fit fermentation

"Say if it's too strong for you . . ."

lock and place in a temperature of 15-17°C (60-65°F) for the main fermentation. If possible use an opaque coloured jar but if you have only a white or clear glass one, wrap it in brown paper or keep it away from the light, to preserve the wine's glorious ruby colour. You may have to top up a little with cold water. Rack for the first time after three months, refitting air lock, and again into clean coloured bottles when the wine is finished (about two months later).

BLACKBERRY WINE (2)

Ingredients:

2.5kg	(6lb)	blackberries
1.25kg	(2½lb)	sugar
		Yeast
		Pectic enzyme
4 litres	(7 pints)	water

Method:

Wash the berries thoroughly in a colander, then crush them in a bowl and pour over them 4 litres (7 pints) of water, boiling. Allow them to steep for two days, then strain the liquor through a nylon sieve on to the sugar, stir well to dissolve, and add the pectic enzyme. 24 hours later add yeast. Leave for five or six days, well covered, then pour into fermenting jar, filling to shoulder, and fit trap, and thereafter continue as usual. This makes a full-bodied, sweet, wine.

BLACKCURRANT WINE

Ingredients:

1.3kg	(3lb)	blackcurrants
1kg	(2¼lb)	sugar
		Yeast and nutrient
4 litres	(7 pints)	water

Method:

Strip any stems from the fruit and wash it well, crush in a polythene bucket with a wooden spoon, and then proceed as for cherry and blackberry wines.

This makes a pleasant, dry and fairly light table wine. A wine with greater body and correspondingly greater sweetness can be made by increasing the weight of fruit up to 2kg (with 3.5 litres (6 pints) of water) and by using 1.3kg (3lb) of sugar.

In this case pour *all* the water, boiling, over the crushed fruit, allow to stand for 24 hours, then strain off the liquor and add the sugar; ferment, rack and bottle as above.

BROOM

This same recipe can also be used for Coltsfoot and many similar flower wines. It is not now recommended, though, that primroses or cowslips be used for winemaking, owing to their increasing scarcity.

BROOM, COLTSFOOT

The same basic recipe can be used for each of these wines, and the most important single point to note is that it is essential, if a wine of good strength is required, to use yeast nutrient. Since these are "ladies' wines" they may be preferred sweet, and I would suggest using 1.3kg (3lb) of sugar, but anyone preferring a medium or dry wine should reduce this quantity to 1.2kg (2½lb) and 1kg (2lb) respectively. Broom wine is certainly the better for having only 1.2kg (2½lb) of sugar.

Ingredients:
  4 litres   (1 gallon)   broom, coltsfoot (heads only)
  1.3kg   (3lb)   white sugar
  **   2 oranges; 1 lemon**
  **   Yeast; yeast nutrient**
  Water to: 4.5 litres (1 gallon)

Method:
Bring 4 litres (6 pints) of water to the boil and stir the sugar into it, making sure that it is all dissolved. Put the peel of the fruit (but no white pith) into a bowl or polythene bucket and pour the hot syrup over it, then allow the liquor to cool to 20°C (70°F) before adding the flowers, fruit juice, yeast, and yeast nutrient. (If delicate flowers are put into boiling water the wine is usually spoilt). Cover closely, and leave in a warm place for seven days, stirring each day. Then strain through a nylon sieve (or muslin) into a fermenting jar, topping up with cold water to the bottom of the neck, and fit a fermentation lock. Leave it in a warm place for three months, by which time there will be an appreciable and firm yeast deposit. Siphon the wine off the lees into a clean jar for another three months, when it can be racked again, this time into bottles if desired.

BULLACE WINE

Bullaces, or bullace plums, are seen in some gardens, and grow wild in many parts of the country, particularly in the Midlands, but many winemakers, seeing them for the first time, wonder what they are, although rightly sensing that they will make excellent wine. The best description one can give of them is that they are a cross between a plum and a sloe, both in size and appearance.

Ingredients:

1.8kg	**(4lb)**	**bullaces**
1.2kg	**(2½lb)**	**sugar**
225g	**(½lb)**	**raisins**
		Pectic enzyme
		Yeast
		Yeast nutrient

Water to: 4.5 litres (1 gallon)

Method:

Crush the fruit to a pulp with a piece of hardwood and pour over it 3.5 litres (6 pints) of water, boiling. Cover with a cloth until cool, then add the pectic enzyme and leave for five days, stirring once or twice a day. Strain through a nylon sieve, pressing with a wooden spoon to express as much juice as possible, and dissolve the sugar in it. Chop the raisins, put them in a colander, and pour some boiling water over them to sterilise them, then place them in a wide necked fermentation vessel. Add the liquor, the yeast nutrient, and your

chosen yeast, cover the mouth of the jar with a sheet of polythene secured with a rubber band, and leave in a temperature of 17-20°C (65-70°F). When the wine has cleared appreciably and a deposit of yeast has appeared (about two months, usually) strain into fresh jar, top up to bottom of neck with cold water, and fit fermentation trap. Rack once more after a further three months, and bottle. Use opaque or dark glass vessels throughout so that the wine will retain its colour.

CABBAGE WINE

Ingredients:

1kg	(2lb)	cabbage, including stalks
		3 oranges or lemons ($\frac{1}{2}$oz citric acid may be used in lieu)
1kg	(2$\frac{1}{4}$lb)	sugar
450g	(1lb)	crushed wheat, rice or barley
225g	($\frac{1}{2}$lb)	minced raisins (scalded)
250ml	($\frac{1}{2}$ pint)	cold tea
		Activated yeast and nutrient

Water to: 4.5 litres (1 gallon)

Method:
Mince the cabbage (including stalks) together with the grains (which should have been soaked overnight), the scalded raisins and rinds (no pith) from the fruit. Place in fermentation vessel and add sugar, add 4 litres (7 pints) of boiling water and stir to dissolve the sugar. When cool add the cold tea, fruit juices (or citric acid), activated yeast and nutrient. Ferment for seven days, then strain into glass jar. Fit fermentation lock, ferment and rack in the normal way.

CARUM CARVI WINE
(Caraway Seed and Tea)

Ingredients:

30g	(1oz)	packet Caraway Seed
450g	(1lb)	raisins or 500ml (1 pint) grape concentrate
15g	($\frac{1}{2}$oz)	citric acid (or 3 lemons, no pith, in lieu)
1.2k	(2$\frac{1}{2}$lb)	sugar
1 litre		weak tea
		Yeast nutrient and activated wine yeast

34

Method:

Add the Caraway Seed to 3 litres (5 pints 5oz) of boiling water and bring this to the boil with the object of extracting the flavour from the seed. Strain over sugar and stir until dissolved. Chop the raisins and after scalding add to the sugared caraway solution. When cool add the citric acid, cold tea, and introduce the yeast nutrient and activated wine yeast. Ferment on the pulp for seven days, then strain into fermenting vessel and ferment under airlock until it clears, then rack for the first time. Bottle when completely clear, about 3/4 months later.

This is a winner!

Got quite a kick, hasn't it?

CARVI FRUCTUS

Ingredients:

30g	(1oz)	Caraway seeds (Boots the Chemists)
450g	(1lb)	crushed barley, wheat or maize
1kg	(2lb)	green gooseberries or stoned raisins
15g	($\frac{1}{2}$oz)	citric acid or 3 lemons (no pith)
5ml		grape tannin
1.3k	(2$\frac{1}{2}$lb)	sugar
		Yeast nutrient
		Activated yeast

Water to 4.5 litres (1 gallon)

Method:

Pour 3.75 litres (6$\frac{1}{2}$ pints) of boiling water over the Caraway seeds, crushed grains, and sugar. Stir well to dissolve the sugar, then add the crushed fruit. When cool add grape tannin, citric acid, nutrient and activated yeast. Ferment on solids for 7-10 days, stirring well each day then strain into fermentation glass jar, and top up with a little cold water if necessary. Fit airlock and ferment to a finish and rack in the usual way.

CARNATION WINE

Ingredients:

2 litres	(2 quarts)	white "pinks"
1.25kg	(2$\frac{1}{2}$lb)	sugar
		1 orange
		1 lemon
225g	($\frac{1}{2}$lb)	raisins
		Yeast, yeast nutrient

Water to 4.5 litres (1 gallon)

Method:

The delightful scent of these flowers does carry over into the wine and give it a really attractive bouquet which will particularly appeal to ladies (most men seem to prefer less "scented" wines). And it is easy to make . . . put the flower heads into a bucket and pour over them 4 litres (7 pints) of water, boiling. Leave for not more than three days, giving an occasional stir. Then strain, and squeeze out the flowers lightly. Chop the raisins and slice the fruit thinly, and add them, with the sugar and yeast nutrient, to the liquor. Stir well to dissolve the sugar. Finally, add your yeast, a wine yeast or a level teaspoon of granulated yeast. Ferment in a temperature of 17-20°C (65-70°F) for 10 days, keeping your bucket closely covered, then strain into a fermenting bottle and fit airlock. When the wine clears and there is a firm yeast sediment, rack into a clean jar, and keep for another three months, this time corked, before the final bottling. It will be usable after about four months in bottle.

CARROT WINE

Ingredients:

1.5k	**(3¼lb)**	**carrots**
1.2k	**(2½lb)**	**granulated sugar**
		Yeast and nutrient
15g	**(½oz)**	**hops**
Water to 4.5 litres (1 gallon)		

"Perhaps just a LEETLE too acid!"

Method:

Scrub the carrots well and chop them up. Put them in 3 litres (6 pints) of water, bring to the boil, and simmer until tender. Strain the liquid into another saucepan or boiler (throw away or eat the carrots!), and add the sugar and hops. Stir well to dissolve the sugar and just bring the liquor to the boil. Allow to cool. Strain into a bucket through a nylon sieve, and when the temperature has dropped to about 20°C (70°F) add yeast, preferably a pre-activated wine yeast, and some yeast nutrient to "give it a boost." If you are using a one-gallon jar do not fill right up to the bottom of the neck in case the fermentation proves too vigorous; keep a little of the liquor aside in a milk bottle plugged with cotton wool. Keep the jar in a warm place, with an airlock fitted, and after five or six days the ferment will have quietened and it can be topped right up from the bottle. Leave until the wine is clearing and a sediment has formed, then siphon it off the lees. Repeat this two to three months later when the wine is completely clear, and bottle.

CHAMOMILE WINE
(Anthemis nobilis)

Ingredients:

		Chamomile Flowers (18 or so)
1.8kg	**(4lb)**	**carrots (swede or turnip if desired)**
15g	**($\frac{1}{2}$oz)**	**citric acid (or 3 lemons, no pith, in lieu)**
1.25k	**($2\frac{1}{2}$lb)**	**sugar**
		A pinch of grape tannin
		Yeast nutrient and activated wine yeast

Water to 4.5 litres (1 gallon)

Method:

Scrub the roots but do not peel. Slice thinly into 3.4 litres (6 pints) of cold water and boil until tender and strain on to sugar. Stir until dissolved. Pour 1 litre ($1\frac{1}{2}$ pint) of boiling water on to chamomile flowers and steep, as making tea. Add the strained infusion to the sugared root juice, also when cool add the citric acid, cold tea, yeast nutrient and activated wine yeast. Ferment under an airlock until it clears, then rack for the first time. Bottle when completely clear, about 3/4 months later.

10g ($\frac{1}{4}$oz) grated Candied Angelica may be added if desired.

CHERRY WINE (1)

Ingredients:

3kg	**(8lb)**	**black cherries (weighed whole)**
4 litres	**(7 pints)**	**water**
1.5kg	**(3½lb)**	**granulated sugar**
		1 Campden tablet
		Yeast and nutrient

Method:

Weigh the cherries whole, then remove stems, wash and stone fruit. Crush the cherries in a bowl, bring 2.5 litres (4 pints) of the water to the boil and pour over them. Cover closely with a sheet of polythene secured by elastic, or with a thick cloth, and leave for 24 hours. Then

"But I only showed him round."

39

strain the liquor through a nylon sieve, or two thicknesses of muslin, and throw away the pulp, after pressing out as much juice as possible. Bring the other 1.5 litres (3 pints) of water to the boil and dissolve the sugar in it, then add this syrup to the liquid already obtained. When the whole has cooled to 20°C (70°F) (just tepid) add the yeast and nutrient and leave in a bowl or polythene bucket for 10 days, closely covered as before, in a warm place 17-20°C (65-70°F). Transfer it then to a glass fermenting jar, topping up to the bottom of the neck if necessary with cold boiled water, and fit fermentation lock. Leave until all fermentation has ceased, then rack into clean jar. Rack again into bottles about two months later. A delicious, medium-sweet dessert wine.

CHERRY WINE (2)

Ingredients:

2kg	(8lb)	sweet cherries (either black or red)
1.25kg	(2½lb)	white sugar
		Pectic enzyme
		1 Campden tablet
		Yeast
		Yeast nutrient

Water to: 4.5 litres (1 gallon)

Method:

Use only ripe fruit, and avoid any which is mouldy or damaged, or it may spoil the wine. Wash the fruit, chop it, place it in a bowl, and pour 3 litres (5½ pints) of cold water over it. Add the Campden tablet and, 24 hours later, the pectic enzyme. Allow the fruit to steep (well covered) for four days. Then place the sugar in a bowl or crock and strain the juice on to it, either through a nylon sieve, or through a jellybag or heavy cloth, squeezing well to express all possible juice. Stir well to dissolve the sugar, then add the yeast and yeast nutrient and pour into fermenting vessel. Ferment and rack in the usual way, topping up with cold water to the bottom of the neck when the first vigour of the fermentation dies down. Cherry wine made in this way will not have the deepness of colour that is obtained by extracting the juice by using heat, but it will have an infinitely better flavour, that of the fresh fruit, and additional colour can easily be added, if desired, to the finished wine by using a little fresh red fruit juice or purchased cherry colouring.

CHRISTMAS DRINKS

OLD-TIME PUNCH

(10 wine glasses)

Ingredients:

<table>
<tr><td></td><td></td><td>1 bottle of any red wine</td></tr>
<tr><td></td><td></td><td>1 cup granulated sugar</td></tr>
<tr><td></td><td></td><td>1 level tablespoon honey</td></tr>
<tr><td></td><td></td><td>1 lemon</td></tr>
<tr><td></td><td></td><td>Little grated nutmeg</td></tr>
<tr><td>**500ml**</td><td>**(1 pint)**</td><td>hot water</td></tr>
<tr><td></td><td></td><td>2 sliced oranges</td></tr>
<tr><td></td><td></td><td>1 carefully peeled red apple</td></tr>
</table>

Method:

Heat wine with sugar, honey, sliced lemon rounds and grated nutmeg in pan to near boiling point. Add the hot water. Pour over sliced orange and apple rounds in large bowl.

Decorate with whole length of apple peel.

SPICED CIDER COMFORTER

(8 wine glasses)

Ingredients:

> 3 level tablespoons honey
> 1 bottle vintage cider
> Small stick cinnamon
> 1 lemon

Method:

Dissolve honey gently in cider over low heat, add cinnamon, lemon peel and juice. Serve hot.

WINE CUP

Ingredients:

		1 bottle red country wine
		1 lemon (juice only)
150ml	(¼ pint)	gin
280ml	(½ pint)	sherry
		1 siphon soda water

Method:

Mix all the ingredients together, garnish with slices of cucumber and a sprig of mint, and if desired enrich with candied cherries and a little maraschino. The cup should be served roughly at room temperature and should not be allowed to stand longer than unavoidable.

CHE-NA-GRUM

In Cornwall at Christmastide a favourite drink is Che-na-grum, or She-nac-rum – hot, sweetened beer flavoured with rum, grated nutmeg and sometimes ginger, and garnished with slices of lemon.

Method:

Place two lumps of sugar in a tumbler. Add a wine-glass of rum. Fill up the glass with hot boiled beer and float two slices of lemon on top. (Enough for one person).

WASSAIL BOWL

Ingredients:

		3 pints ale
225g	**(½lb)**	**brown sugar**
		½ bottle sherry of Madeira
		6 roasted apples
60g	**(½oz)**	**ground ginger**
		½ grated nutmeg
		Pinch of ground cinnamon
		2 lumps of sugar
		1 washed lemon
		½ lemon

Method:

Prepare the apples first. Core them, stuff with brown sugar, and roast in a covered dish for 20 minutes, then uncover, baste, and finish cooking. Mix the spices with the sugar. Place in an enamel saucepan; add 1 pint ale. Stir over low heat till dissolved, then bring to boil, draw pan to side of stove. Stir in remainder of ale, the sherry of Madeira, and the sugar, rubbed on to the lemon until all the oil is extracted. Heat till piping hot, but do not allow to boil. Pour into a hot, ornamental bowl. Add the hot, roasted, stuffed apples, then the half lemon, peeled so that all the white pith has been removed, and cut in slices. Place the bowl on a cake board or salver, and ornament round the base with holly or mistletoe. Serve at once with a ladle.

ALE PUNCH

Ingredients:

55g	**(2oz)**	**castor sugar**
		1 lemon
		2 quarts light ale
280ml	**(½ pint)**	**sherry**
		6 ice blocks

Method:

Place the sugar in a punch bowl. Wash the lemon. Remove rind as thinly as possible and add to sugar. Extract lemon juice and strain over the sugar. Stand for ½ hour, then remove lemon rind. Add ale, sherry and ice. Garnish with 1 or 2 slices of lemon. Enough for six or seven persons.

CLARY WINE

This is a favourite wine in many parts of the country, and is made from the blue flowers of Clary Sage. Clary is a member of the sage family, and the blue blossoms are gathered if possible just before they show signs of deteriorating, which is generally in late summer. (Beekeepers: the Clary Sage is reputed to be a good "bee" plant and is a useful source of nectar as well as pollen). This recipe will make a medium-sweet, delicate wine.

Ingredients:
 1.5 litres (3 pints)   **Clary sage blossom**
                                  (or 1 pkt dried blossom)
 1.25kg   **(2¾lb)**   **sugar**
 450g   **(1lb)**   **raisins**
                                  2 lemons
                                  Yeast; yeast nutrient
 Water to: 4.5 litres (1 gallon)

"No thanks; I have my own."

Method:

If you are using the dried blossoms obtained from a herbalist it will be necessary to infuse for 24 hours before use. Boil the sugar in 3.5 litres (6 pints) of water for a few minutes and ensure that it is all well dissolved, then pour the hot liquor over the clary blossoms, the chopped raisins, and the juice and thin rinds (no pith) of the lemons. When the temperature has dropped to 20°C (70°F), add the yeast, a wine yeast or a level teaspoon of granulated yeast, and some yeast nutrient. Cover closely and stand in a warm place for a week to ferment. Stir well each day. After that period, remove the flowers, but leave the raisins in the liquor for a further 10 days before straining into a fermenting jar, topping up with cold water, and fitting trap. Rack the wine for the first time when the top half is clear, and again about two months later when it has cleared completely.

COFFEE WINE
(by W. Beavis, Southend)

Ingredients:

1 tablespoon	Nescafe
1.25kg (2½lb)	sugar
	2 lemons
	Yeast and nutrient

Water to: 4.5 litres (1 gallon)

Method:

Peel the lemons thinly, avoiding the white pith (a grater is the ideal way) and boil the peel in 3.5 litres (6½ pints) of water with the coffee for half an hour. Strain on to the sugar and stir well to dissolve, allow to cool, and add the yeast, nutrient, and strained juice of the lemons. Cover closely and leave in a temperature of 15-17C° (65-70°F) for about a week, before transferring to a 1-gallon fermenting jar and fitting air lock. Top up with cold boiled water or syrup. Leave to ferment right out, then transfer to a cool place 13°C (55-60°F) and siphon off the lees into clean bottles when it is completely clear.

COLTSFOOT
(See Broom)

CONCENTRATED FRUIT JUICES

Several readers have asked for recipes for using some of the fruit juice concentrates now available, so here are some they may care to try:

CIDER or PERRY 25 litres (5 gallons): (SG 60). Use 4.5 litres (1 gallon) Concentrated Apple or Pear Juice. Use a reliable yeast nutrient, Steinberg, Champagne, All-purpose, Kaltgarhefe, or Perlschaum Yeast.

"Just a little YOUNG, perhaps?"

LIGHT APPLE or PEAR WINE (SG 100) 25 litres (5 gallons): Use 4.5 litres (1 gallon) Concentrated Apple or Pear Juice, 13 litres (3 gallons) water and 2.4kg (5lb 6oz) sugar dissolved initially in 2.8 litres (5 pints) water. Use a good yeast nutrient and Perlschaum, Rudesheimer, Tokay, All-purpose or Cold Fermentation Yeast.

HEAVY SWEET APPLE or PEAR WINE (SG 150): 4.5 litres (1 gallon) of Concentrated Apple or Pear Juice plus 11 litres (2½ gallons) of water. Make first a syrup by dissolving 8.5kg (12lb) of sugar in 3.5 litres (6 pints) of the water. Add one-third of this syrup to the must and ferment with Sauternes, Tokay, All-purpose or Sherry Yeast with a good nutrient. Add the remainder of the syrup in two doses at suitable intervals, when the fermentation slows. To make 4.5 litres (1 gallon) adjust ingredients accordingly.

CYSER ("Melomel"): Substitute 570ml (1 pint) Apple Juice, concentrate for 450g (1lb) honey per gallon in any mead recipe and reduce any added acid recommended by at least ¼oz per gallon.

RHUBARB AND APPLE: Substitute 570ml (1 pint) concentrate for 450g (1lb) of sugar per gallon in any rhubarb recipe and reduce any added acid recommended by at least ¼oz per gallon.

CRAB APPLE WINE (1)

Ingredients:

4kg	(10-12lb)	crab apples
150ml		grape concentrate (or 500g raisins)
450g	(1lb)	wheat
1kg	(2¼lb)	sugar
		Yeast, yeast nutrient
		Pectic enzyme

Water to: 4.5 litres (1 gallon)

Method:

Wash the crab apples, then chop or crush them, and cover them with 3.7 litres (6½ pints) of water. Add the pectic enzyme, a level teaspoon of granulated yeast and some yeast nutrient and stir well in. Cover closely and leave in a warm place about 20°C (70°F), stirring well each day and mashing the apples with the hand, for 7 days.

By this time the yeast will be fully active and much increased, so stir well, then strain through a nylon sieve. Enough yeast will be carried over to continue the ferment. Stir in the sugar, the grape concentrate or the chopped raisins, and the wheat, cover closely, and leave in a warm place to ferment for 14 days. Then strain into a fermenting jar, top with cold water, and fit airlock. Leave until the wine clears and there is a firm sediment, then siphon it off the lees into a fresh jar and refit trap. Leave for a further three months before racking again, this time into clean bottles.

CRAB APPLE WINE (2)

Ingredients:

3.6kg	(8lb)	crab apples
1.3kg	(2¾lb)	sugar
4.5 litres	(1 gallon)	water
		Yeast, yeast nutrient
		Pectic enzyme

"There MUST be an easier way!"

Method:

Put the crab apples in 3.7 litres (6½ pints) of water and leave for three or four days (until they are well soaked) then mash them with the hand or a hardwood pulper and add the pectic enzyme, yeast and nutrient. Leave another fortnight (closely covered, of course) stirring daily, then strain the liquor on to the sugar and stir well to dissolve. If you have any kind of press it pays dividends to extract all possible juice from the pulp. Stir well to dissolve all the sugar, put into fermenting jar, and fit trap. Top up if necessary. Siphon off the lees when clear into clean bottles.

CURRANT WINE

Ingredients:

1.3kg	(3lb)	**currants**
225g	(½lb)	**mixed minced peel**
225g	(½lb)	**barley**
1.25kg	(2½lb)	**sugar**
		Yeast; nutrient

Water to: 4.5 litres (1 gallon)

Method:

Bring 3.5 litres (6 pints) of water to the boil, add the currants, peel and barley, and simmer for 15 minutes. Strain on to the sugar and stir well to dissolve. When the liquor has cooled to 20°C (70°F) – tepid – add a vigorous yeast and yeast nutrient, pour the whole into a fermenting jar and fit trap. When the first frothy vigour of the ferment dies down "top-up" with cold water to the bottom of the neck. Leave to ferment out, and siphon off the lees when it clears. Refit trap and leave till wine is stable; then bottle.

CURRANT AND RAISIN WINE

Ingredients:

900g	(2lb)	**currants**
900g	(2lb)	**raisins**
		1 orange
		1 lemon
450g	(1lb)	**rice**
1.2kg	(2¾lb)	**sugar**
		Yeast; nutrient
4.5 litres (1 gallon)		**water**

Method:

Bring the 3.5 litres (6 pints) of water to the boil, add the currants, raisins, and orange peel, and simmer for 20 minutes. Strain, add the rice, and simmer for four minutes. Strain on to the sugar and stir thoroughly to dissolve it, and when the liquor has cooled to 20°C (70°F) add the juice of the orange and lemon, the yeast, and some yeast nutrient. Pour into fermenting jar and fit air lock, ferment out, rack and bottle in the usual way. A variation is to use 1.8kg (4lb) currants, 450g (1lb) raisins, 1kg (2¼lb) sugar, this will give a drier wine.

DAMSON WINE

Beware of recipes which you will find in some books which tell you to boil damsons, for if you overdo it you will release pectin into the wine, which will either jellify or prove almost impossible to clear, the commonest fault with plum wines. Far better just to pour the boiling water over the fruit.

"Just a little invention of my own."

Ingredients:
1.8kg	**(4lb)**	**damsons or**
2.7kg	**(6lb)**	**for really good body**
1.3kg	**(3lb)**	**sugar**
		Yeast
		Yeast nutrient
		Pectic enzyme

Water to: 4.5 litres (1 gallon)

Method:
Put 3.5 litres (6 pints) of water on to boil, then crush the damsons in a bowl or bucket with half the sugar. Pour the boiling water over them, stir really well dissolve the sugar, and allow to cool to about 25°C (75°F) before adding the pectic enzyme, yeast and yeast nutrient. Cover closely and leave for 48 hours in a warm place to allow the ferment to get well under way. Put the remaining sugar in a polythene bucket or other vessel and strain the liquor on to it. In this case a nylon sieve or muslin is often not fine enough and it pays to use a jelly bag or roll the pulp to and fro in nylon netting to be sure of the wine clearing.

And do not try to force out the last of the juice, or again you will cloud the wine: give it time to run through naturally and this is where the pectic enzyme helps. It pays to be patient here. Stir well to make sure that all sugar is thoroughly dissolved, then pour into fermenting jar and top up with cold water. Fit trap and allow ferment to finish. (It may be slow getting going again after you have used the jellybag or otherwise strained it thoroughly but do not worry about this; enough yeast will pass through to cause a ferment, but you must give it time to multiply again.) Rack when the wine is really clear, and again three months later if a second yeast deposit is thrown. Then bottle in dark bottles. A beautiful, satisfying wine, this.

DANDELION WINE

Above all, in Spring, do not neglect to make dandelion wine, for it is an excellent accompaniment for fish and poultry, and will not disgrace anyone's table. Three trade secrets: (1) Use the right quantity of flowers; (2) Make sure the blooms are fully open; and (3) whatever you do, do not soak them above three days, or the wine will have a foul bouquet.

Ingredients:

3 litres	**(3 quarts)**	**flowers**
1.2kg	**(2lb 11oz)**	**sugar**
		2 lemons
		1 orange
		Yeast
		150ml grape concentrate or 450g (1lb) raisins

Water to: 4.5 litres (1 gallon)

Method:

Gather the flowers on a sunny day, when they are fully open (traditionally St. George's Day, 23rd April, is the time) and make your wine the same day, whilst they are fresh. Pick the heads off the stalks, leaving as little stalk as possible; there is no need to pick off individual petals, as some advocate. Put the blooms into a polythene bucket, and pour 7 pints of water, boiling, over them. Leave for three days (this is the absolute maximum, and two will do) stirring each

Happy birthday, dear.

53

day, and keeping the bowl closely covered. Then strain the whole into a boiler, and add the sugar and the rinds of the lemon and orange, from which you have extracted the juice. Do not include any white pith. Boil for an hour, then return to the bucket, and add the juice of the lemons and orange. Allow to cool to 20°C (70°F), then add a good wine yeast, or a level teaspoon of granulated yeast, and some yeast nutrient, since this is a liquor likely to be deficient in desirable elements. Keep the bucket closely covered for three days in a warm place, then strain into a fermenting jar and add the concentrate or raisins before fitting a fermentation lock. Leave until the wine clears, then rack, through a sieve, into a clean jar, and leave till Christmas, by which time this wine is usually fit to drink. Another six months' storage, however (particularly in a cask), will bring a noticeable improvement.

DATE WINE

This is a variation upon one of the old-fashioned recipes, but a good one, despite the variety of ingredients:

Ingredients:

450g	(1lb)	dates
225g	($\frac{1}{2}$lb)	barley
		1 orange
		1 lemon
1kg	(2$\frac{1}{4}$lb)	sugar
		$\frac{1}{2}$ nutmeg
		Yeast; yeast nutrient

Water to: 4.5 litres (1 gallon)

Method:

Chop up the dates and slice the orange and lemon. Boil the barley in 4 litres (7 pints) of water for 10 minutes, then strain on to the dates and citrus fruit; add the half nutmeg (it should not be grated). Simmer for 12 minutes, then strain on to the sugar, and stir well to dissolve. Cool to 20°C (70°F), add the yeast and nutrient, and keep in a warm place, closely covered, for five days, stirring daily. Then pour into fermenting jar, top up with cold water, and fit fermentation lock. Leave until it begins to clear, then rack and move into a cooler place. Rack into clean bottles when completely clear and stable.

DATE AND APRICOT WINE

Ingredients:

900g	**(2lb)**	**dates**
450g	**(1lb)**	**dried apricots**
225g	**(½lb)**	**barley (if desired)**
1.2kg	**(2lb 11oz)**	**sugar**
		2 oranges
		2 lemons
		Yeast; nutrient

Water to 4.5 litres (1 gallon)

Method:

Peel the citrus fruit and chop the dates. Bring 3.5 litres (6 pints) of water to the boil, and add the fruit, citrus peel, and barley if used (barley lends body to the wine but alters the true flavour). Simmer for 10 minutes, then strain on to the sugar and juice of the oranges and lemons. Stir well, allow to cool to 20°C (70°F), then pour into fermentation jar and add yeast and nutrient; fit fermentation lock. Top up with water when ferment slows and ferment right out in the usual way. Rack when it first clears, and bottle three months later. A variation is to use 3lb dates and omit the apricots.

ELDERBERRY – AND BILBERRY – WITH VARIATIONS

Elderberries are excellent for making "the Englishman's port", as the wine from them is sometimes called; indeed, at one time, until the practice was made illegal, elderberries were used to improve true port. Some winemakers are occasionally disappointed in their elderberry wine because it seems unduly harsh and dry, so much so as to be almost undrinkable young, but if the wine is matured sufficiently (sometimes it needs two years) this harshness, caused by the excess tannin in this fruit, disappears. If you cannot resist drinking your elderberry wine young, the addition of a little sugar just before use effects a near-miraculous improvement!

In all the following recipes, whether for fresh or dried fruit, **bilberries** can be substituted for elderberries. They too make a glorious wine, the flavour of which many prefer to that of the elderberry.

ECSTATIC ELDERBERRY

Ingredients:

1.8kg	(4lb)	elderberries
1.25kg	(2lb 11oz)	sugar
		Burgundy yeast; nutrient
20g	($\frac{1}{2}$oz)	citric acid
Water to 4.5 litres (1 gallon)		

Method:

To strip the berries from the stalks wear rubber gloves or use the prongs of a fork or steel comb, otherwise it is a messy and tedious business. And be careful that drops of the juice do not stain your clothes because the mark seems to resist all subsequent attempts to remove it. Weigh the berries (together with any other fruit recommended in the variation recipes) and crush them in a bowl or bucket. If grape concentrate is being used it is added at this stage. Pour on 3.5 litres (6 pints) of boiling water, stir well, and allow to cool to 20°C (70°F) before adding the yeast, acid, and nutrient. Cover closely and leave for three days in a warm place, stirring daily, then strain through a nylon sieve on to the sugar. Pour the liquor into a stone jar or dark glass jar (in clear bottles the wine will lose its glorious ruby colour) but do not fill completely until the first vigorous ferment has subsided; when it has, top up with cold boiled water and fit fermentation lock. Leave till fermentation is complete, then siphon off into clean dark bottles (if you have no dark bottles cover your white ones with a sugar bag or brown paper, or keep them in a dark cupboard) and keep for a further six months at least.

"Do hurry up with the wine, dear, the guests are arriving . . . . ."

(2) ELDERBERRY ENCHANT

Ingredients:

1.8kg	**(4lb)**	**elderberries**
1.25kg	**(2¾lb)**	**white sugar**
150ml		**grape concentrate**
20g	**(½oz)**	**citric acid**
		Wine yeast culture and nutrient

Water to: 4.5 litres (1 gallon)

Method:

As basic recipe above, except that grape concentrate is added to the "must". This gives a slightly stronger wine, with a more vinous "nose".

(3) NON PAREIL

(from a French recipe)

Ingredients:

1.3kg	**(3lb)**	**elderberries**
450g	**(1lb)**	**damsons**
1.2kg	**(2¾lb)**	**sugar**
20g	**(½oz)**	**citric acid**
		Wine yeast culture and nutrient

Water to: 4.5 litres (1 gallon)

Method:

As for Basic Recipe.

(4) "AMBROSIA"

(an eighteenth century recipe)

Ingredients:

1.3kg	**(3lb)**	**elderberries**
450g	**(1lb)**	**raisins**
		root ginger and cloves
1.25kg	**(2¾lb)**	**sugar**
20g	**(½oz)**	**citric acid**
		Wine yeast culture and nutrient

Method:

Boil the root ginger and cloves in the water whilst bringing it to the boil; simmer for 15 minutes. Add the stoned raisins, then continue as indicated in basic recipe. The inclusion of the root ginger and cloves is optional and may be omitted if desired, but was greatly liked in olden days, when spicy flavours were popular.

(5) CREME DE RAISIN

Ingredients:

1.3kg	(3lb)	elderberries
1.8kg	(4lb)	grapes or 570ml (1 pint) grape concentrate
1kg	(2¼lb)	sugar
15g	(½oz)	citric acid
		Wine yeast culture and nutrient

Method:
As for Basic Recipe.

(6) VINO MAGNIFICO

Ingredients:

1.2kg	(3lb)	elderberries
450g	(1lb)	sloes
150ml		grape concentrate
1kg	(2¼lb)	sugar
15g	(½oz)	citric acid
		Wine yeast culture and nutrient

Method:
As for Basic Recipe.

"I think I use rather too much of the main ingredient."

(7) ELDERBERRY AND APPLE

Ingredients:

1.3kg	(3lb)	elderberries
1.8kg	(4lb)	apples
1kg	(2¼lb)	sugar
15g	(½oz)	citric acid
		Yeast culture and nutrient

Method:

Wash and cut up the apples and boil 10-15 minutes in 4 litres (7 pints) of water; then strain on to elderberries and proceed as for Basic Recipe.

(8) AS YOU LIKE IT

Ingredients:

900g	(2lb)	elderberries
900g	(2lb)	blackberries
1.2kg	(2½lb)	sugar
30g	(1oz)	citric acid
		Wine yeast culture and nutrient

Method:

As for Basic Recipe.

(9) AROMATIC SPLENDOUR

Ingredients:

1.8kg	(4lb)	elderberries
		1 flagon commercial cider (or more)
20g	(½oz)	citric acid
		Yeast culture and nutrient
900g	(2lb)	sugar

Method:

Reduce the amount of water being used by the amount of cider added and proceed as for Basic Recipe.

(10) HERBAL NECTAR

Ingredients:

30g	(1oz)	of mixed herbs
1.8kg	(4lb)	elderberries
15g	(½oz)	citric acid
		Yeast culture and nutrient

Method:
Proceed as for Basic Recipe.

ELDERBERRY (Dried) AND BANANA
(see under Banana)

(11) ELDERBERRY WINE
(from dried elderberries or bilberries)

Ingredients:

450g	(1lb)	dried elderberries
		(equals 4lb of fresh fruit)
1kg	(2¼lb)	sugar
200ml		grape concentrate
		1 lemon
		Yeast and yeast nutrient

Water to: 4.5 litres (1 gallon)

"I think he
found it
quite a
tonic!"

Method:

Bring 4 litres (7 pints) of water to the boil, and pour over the dried elderberries, 500g sugar, concentrate and lemon juice, in polythene bucket. Stir well and cover. Allow to cool to 20°C (70°F), then add the yeast and yeast nutrient. A Bordeaux, Port, or Burgundy yeast is excellent. Ferment on the pulp for a week before straining through a nylon sieve or muslin into the fermenting jar, add remaining sugar, and make up to 4.5 litres (1 gallon). Stir well to dissolve. Fit an air lock, and ferment in the usual way. Rack for the first time when the wine clears and again three months later.

The same recipe can be used for bilberries.

ELECAMPANE WINE
(Inula Helenium)

"The wine wherein the root of Elecampane hath steept is singular good against colicke" – Markham, *Country Farme*, A.D. 1616

Ingredients:

		1 small packet Elecampane Herb
		1 marrow (1-1.5kg) (2-3lb)
15g	($\frac{1}{2}$oz)	citric acid (or 3 lemons, no pith, in lieu)
1.3kg	(3lb)	sugar
		A pinch of grape tannin
		Yeast nutrient and activated wine yeast

Water to: 4.5 litres (1 gallon)

Method:

Pour 3.5 litres (6 pints) boiling water over the grated or sliced marrow, including the seeds, and leave this, well covered, to soak for 24 hours. Then pour 570ml (1 pint) of boiling water over the Elecampane herb and infuse as for tea. Strain over sugar, add the strained marrow infusion, the citric acid and tannin, and stir well until all is dissolved. When cool, add the yeast nutrient and activated yeast, make up to one gallon when the ferment slows. Ferment under an air lock until it clears, then rack for the first time. Bottle when completely clear about four months later.

FENNEL WINE
(Foeniculum vulgare)

"It is much used in drink to make people more lean that are too fat." – Culpeper.

Ingredients:

		1 small packet Fennel Herb
1.3kg	(3lb)	beetroot
1.25kg	(2lb)	sugar
15g	($\frac{1}{2}$oz)	citric acid (or 3 lemons, no pith, in lieu)
250ml	($\frac{1}{2}$ pint)	cold strong tea (or a pinch of grape tannin)
		Yeast nutrient and activated wine yeast

Water to: 4.5 litres (1 gallon)

Method:

Wash the beetroot well and slice thinly, then boil in 3.5 litres (6 pints) of water until slightly tender; strain on to the sugar. Pour 250ml ($\frac{1}{2}$ pint) of boiling water over the fennel herb and infuse as for tea. Strain on to sugared beetroot juice. When cool add the citric acid, cold tea, yeast nutrient and activated wine yeast. Ferment under an air lock, topping up with cold water when the ferment quietens, until it clears, then rack for the first time. Bottle when completely clear, about 3/4 months later.

FIG WINE

Ingredients:
1kg	(2lb)	dried figs
1.25kg	(2lb 11oz)	sugar
		1 orange
		1 lemon

Water to: 4.5 litres (1 gallon)

Method:
Soak the figs overnight in a little cold water, then make the quantity up to 3.5 litres (6 pints), bring to the boil, and simmer for five minutes. Strain on to the sugar, stir well to dissolve and top up to shoulder of jar. Add the juice of the citrus fruit. When cool 20°C (70°F) add the yeast and nutrient and ferment under an air lock in the usual way topping up to bottom of neck with cold water as fermentation slows. It will usually take about three months to clear, when it can be racked, and another two months to be ready for bottling. This is a dry wine well worth making.

FIG AND BANANA
(see under Banana)

FIG AND SULTANA (GOLDEN GLOW)

Ingredients:
1kg	(2lb)	Demerara sugar
1kg	(2lb)	sultanas
1kg	(2lb)	figs
225g	(8oz)	barley
		Yeast; yeast nutrient

Water to: 4.5 litres (1 gallon)

Method:
This makes a wine of good colour and body, and about 12% alcohol. Put the barley to soak overnight in 280ml (half a pint) of water. The next day mince the barley and chop the sultanas and fruit, dropping them into a polythene bucket or crock. Meanwhile bring 3.75 litres (6½ pints) of water to the boil. Pour it, boiling, over the grain and fruit, and stir in the sugar. Allow to cool to 20°C (70°F), then add the yeast and yeast nutrient (a sherry or sauternes yeast is excellent, but failing that use a level teaspoon of granulated yeast). Ferment on the pulp for 10 days, stirring once a day, then strain

through a nylon sieve or two thicknesses of muslin into a fermenting jar and fit air lock, topping up to within 20mm ($\frac{3}{4}$ in) of the bottom of the cork with cold boiled water if necessary. Ferment out and rack when it clears (about eight weeks). Rack again after a further two months or so into clean bottles.

FIG AND PARSNIP
(see Parsnip and Fig)

FRUIT JUICES
(Using, see under "Concentrated Fruit Juices")

"Her Ladyship used some of her own gooseberry champagne..."

65

GINGER WINE

Ingredients:

80g	(3oz)	root ginger
		2 oranges
		2 lemons
225g	($\frac{1}{2}$lb)	raisins
1.3kg	(3lb)	sugar
		Yeast; yeast nutrient

Water to: 4.5 litres (1 gallon)

Method:

Peel the fruit thinly, avoiding the white pith, and put the peel and juice of the oranges and lemons into a bucket or bowl, with the chopped raisins. Bring 3.5 litres (6 pints) of water to the boil, and add to it the sugar and ginger, well crushed. Boil for half-an-hour, and make up if necessary to about 4 litres (6 pints). Bring it to the boil again, and pour on to the rinds and fruit. Then allow the liquor to cool to 20°C (70°F), (this can be speeded up by standing the bucket in cold water after the first ten minutes). Add the yeast and yeast nutrient, cover and leave in a warm 17°-20°C (65°-70°F), place for 10 days or so. Next, strain into a fermenting jar, top up, and fit air lock. Bottle when it clears and fermentation is finished.

GINGER GLOW

Ingredients:

1.25kg	(2lb 11oz)	sugar
15g	($\frac{1}{2}$oz)	essence ginger
15g	($\frac{1}{2}$oz)	essence cayenne
15g	($\frac{1}{2}$oz)	burnt sugar or 500ml (1 pint) strong tea
15g	($\frac{1}{2}$oz)	tartaric acid
		Yeast and nutrient

Water to: 4.5 litres (1 gallon)

Method:

Put the sugar in fermenting bucket; add 3.5 litres boiling water to dissolve sugar. When cool add the essences, etc., and introduce yeast and nutrient. Fit lock and ferment in usual way, topping up as necessary with cold water.

GOATS-BEARD WINE

(Tragopogon-Pratensis)
(by C. Shave)

Found in meadows, the yellow flowered goats-beard has a folk name "John go to bed at noon" due to the fact that its flowers open at 4 o'clock in the morning and close by noon. It flowers throughout June and July.

Ingredients:

4.5 litres	(1 gallon)	Goats-beard flowers
1.3kg	(3lb)	sugar
5ml	(1 teaspoon)	grape tannin
		2 lemons or 20g ($\frac{1}{2}$oz) citric acid
		Activated yeast and nutrient

Water to: 4.5 litres (1 gallon)

Method:

Remove stalks and put the flowers into a polythene bucket jar with the grated lemon rinds (no pith) and sugar. Pour on 3.5 litres (6 pints) boiling water, stir to dissolve the sugar and leave to cool. Add cold tea, lemon juice or citric acid, activated yeast and yeast nutrient. Cover bucket and leave for two days, then strain into fermenting jar, top up to bottom of neck with cold water and fit air lock. Ferment out and bottle in usual way.

GOLDEN ROD WINE

"True love lies bleeding, with the hearts-at-ease:
And Golden Rods, and tansy running high
That o'er the pale top smiled on passer-by."

(JOHN CLARE)

Most gardens, if they have any at all, have a profusion of blooms of golden rod, and these will make an excellent wine, particularly, if it is made not too sweet: it is a glorious golden colour.

Ingredients :

570ml	(1 pint)	blossom (not pressed down)
850g	(1¾lb)	white sugar
225g	(½lb)	raisins
		6 sweet oranges
		Yeast; yeast nutrient

Water to: 4.5 litres (1 gallon)

Method:

Bring 3.5 litres (6 pints) of water to the boil and dissolve the sugar in it, stirring for a minute or two to ensure that this is complete; then pour the boiling syrup over the flowers and raisins and add the orange juice. Allow the liquor to cool to 20°C (70°F), then add the yeast and the yeast nutrient, and leave to stand for five days, covered closely, in a temperature of about 17°C (65°F). Give it a good stir from the bottom once or twice daily. Then strain into a jar, filling it to just below the bottom of the neck, and fit a fermentation lock. When the wine has noticeably cleared, and there is an appreciable deposit, rack into a clean jar; repeat the racking three to four months later, this time into bottles. The wine will be at its best about six months later.

GRAPE AND SULTANA

Ingredients :

450g	(1lb)	sultanas
450g	(1lb)	grapes
850g	(1¾lb)	sugar
225g	(8oz)	barley
		Yeast and nutrient

Water to: 4.5 litres (1 gallon)

68

Method:

Soak the barley overnight in half a pint of (extra) water and the next day mince both grain and sultanas. Bring 3.5 litres (6 pints) of water to the boil and pour it over the grain and fruit, then crush the grapes manually and add. Stir in the sugar and make sure that it is all dissolved. Allow to cool until just tepid 20°C (70°F), then introduce the yeast, preferably a sherry yeast, and nutrient, and ferment, closely covered, for 10 days, stirring daily. Strain into fermenting jar, top up with a little cold water, fit air lock and ferment out in the usual way, racking when clear, and bottling after a further two months.

"Not when you're wearing that old lace pinny — I've seen the play!"

GREENGAGE WINE

Plums are commonly used for wine, and it is puzzling that greengages are not more popular for the purpose, for they make a wine which many think superior in both taste and appearance to that made from "blue" plums which often has an unattractive colour. Do not neglect to use a pectic enzyme for this wine.

Ingredients:

2kg	**(4lb)**	**greengages**
1.3kg	**(3lb)**	**sugar**
		Yeast and nutrient
		Pectic enzyme

Water to: 4.5 litres (1 gallon)

Method:

Cut up the greengages and pour 3.5 litres (6 pints) of boiling water over them. Let it cool considerably before adding the pectic enzyme. Keep well covered for four days, mashing the fruit with the hands and stirring it well each day.

Then strain the liquor on to the sugar, add the yeast and nutrient, and transfer to fermentation jar with trap. It is best to use a vigorously fermenting yeast starter and to start the fermentation (for three days at least) at a comparatively high temperature, between 20-25°C (70-75°F). Then reduce it to 17°C (65°F), and top up with cold water to bottom of neck. Rack the wine when it clears, and repeat the process two or three months later. This is a clean, medium-sweet wine, most useful for table purposes.

HAWTHORNBERRY WINE

Ingredients:

4.5 litres (1 gallon)		**hawthornberries**
1.2kg	**(2lb 10oz)**	**white sugar**
		2 lemons
		Yeast and nutrient

Water to: 4.5 litres (1 gallon)

Method:

Wash the berries in a colander under a running tap and then place them in a bowl or crock, and bruise them with a stainless steel spoon or piece of hardwood. Pour over them 3.5 litres (6 pints) water (cold) and add the juice and thin peel of the lemons, being careful to exclude any white pith, which will give the wine a distinctly bitter taste.

Cover your bucket closely with a folded towel and leave it for five or six days, so that the flavour can be drawn from the berries. Do not forget to give it a daily stir. Then strain on to the sugar and stir well to dissolve it. Finally add your yeast and the requisite amount of any yeast nutrient, and stir well in. Pour the yeasted liquor into a fermenting jar, filling it to the shoulder, fit an air lock. Fit fermentation trap and keep the jar in a warm place 17-20°C (65-70°F). After a week or so the ferment will have quietened and the fermenting jar can then be "topped up" as full as possible with cold water, and the trap refitted. When the wine clears and a good yeast sediment has formed rack for the first time (this is usually after $2\frac{1}{2}$-3 months) and again, into bottles, two months later. This is distinctive and agreeable table wine.

"But it's just full of vitamin C."

HERBAL DELIGHT

(By C. S. Shave)

Ingredients:

		1 tablespoon mixed herbs
225g	**($\frac{1}{2}$oz)**	**citric acid**
280ml	**($\frac{1}{2}$ pint)**	**stewed tea**
1.3kg	**(3lb)**	**sugar**
3.5 litres (6 pints)		**water**
		Yeast; yeast nutrient

Method:

Dissolve 1kg (2lb) sugar in 3.5 litres (6 pints) of boiling water and pour over the herbs; add the citric acid, stewed tea. When cool add yeast, and yeast nutrient, and leave to ferment for 48 hours in a warm place. Strain. Then top up with the remaining sugar. Fit fermentation lock and ferment to completion. The wine should be racked (i.e. siphoned off the yeast deposit after about $3\frac{1}{2}$ months).

HUCKLEBERRY WINE

(Solanum nigrum var. Guineense)

Ingredients:

1.3kg	**(3lb)**	**garden huckleberries**
1.2kg	**(2lb 11oz)**	**sugar**
		Yeast and nutrient
Water to: 4.5 litres (1 gallon)		

Method:

Pick the berries when they are fully ripe and crush them in a bowl with a stainless steel spoon. Add 3.5 litres (6 pints) of water and mix thoroughly. Allow to stand overnight, then strain through a nylon sieve on to the sugar, and stir well to dissolve. Add yeast and nutrient, cover closely with a sheet of polythene or thick cloth, and leave in a warm place, 17-20°C (70-75°F) for a week. When first vigorous ferment subsides stir, and transfer to fermenting jar. Fit fermentation lock and place in temperature of 15-17°C (60-65°F) for the main fermentation. Top up with cold water as necessary. If possible use a coloured or opaque jar to keep out the light, or wrap your clear glass jar with brown paper. Rack for first time after three months, refit air lock, and rack again into clean bottles after a further three months.

KOHL RABI WINE

Ingredients:

2kg	**4lb**	**Kohl Rabi** (early Purple Vienna variety was grown)
		1 orange or 15g ($\frac{1}{2}$oz) citric acid
		1 lemon
1.25kg	**(2lb 11oz)**	**sugar**
		Yeast; nutrient

Method:

Scrub the roots well – it is not necessary to peel them – and cut them into 6mm ($\frac{1}{4}$in) slices. Put them into a large saucepan or boiler in 3 litres (5 pints 5oz) of water, bring to the boil, and simmer until tender. Do not, however, allow them to go mushy or the wine will not clear subsequently. Strain the liquor on to the sliced fruit and sugar. Simmer for half an hour, stirring well for the first few minutes, then strain through a nylon sieve into a fermenting jar and allow to cool to 21°C (70°F) before adding your yeast and nutrient. Plug jar with cotton wool for the first four days until the fermentation quietens, then top up with 500-700ml (1 pint) cold water and fit air lock. After a week move into a slightly lower temperature and after three months the wine should be clearing and can be racked, or siphoned, into a clean bottle, leaving the sediment behind. Refit air lock and leave for a further three months; then rack again, this time into wine bottles, and cork securely. The same recipe can be used for turnip wine.

"Anyone seen my hydrometer?"

LAVENDER

Ingredients:

1 litre	(2 pints)	lavender leaves (no stalk)
200ml		grape concentrate
1.25kg	(2lb 12oz)	sugar
15g	($\frac{1}{2}$oz)	citric acid (or 3 lemons, no pith)
250ml	($\frac{1}{2}$ pint)	cold strong tea or pinch of grape tannin
		Yeast nutrient
		Activated yeast

Water to: 4.5 litres (1 gallon)

Method:

Pour 3.5 litres (6 pints) of boiling water over the lavender leaves and steep for 24 hours. Then strain over the sugar and concentrate and stir until all is dissolved, warming the liquor gently meanwhile. Cool to 20°C (70°F) and add the tannin or cold tea, acid, yeast and nutrient. Fit air lock and ferment, rack and bottle as usual.

LIMEFLOWER

(by C. S. Shave)

Ingredients:

		4 full teaspoons Limeflower tea
450g	(1lb)	chopped raisins
1.3kg	(2lb 12oz)	sugar
		2 lemons
		2 oranges or 15g ($\frac{1}{2}$oz) citric acid
		Yeast nutrient
		Yeast (selected wine)

Water to: 4.5 litres (1 gallon)

Method:

Infuse the tea in 3.5 litres (6 pints) boiling water and leave to stand 24 hours, strain, and simmer with raisins, grated orange and lemon peel (no pith). Strain on to sugar and add fruit juices or citric acid. When cool add yeast nutrient, introduce activated wine yeast and allow fermentation to proceed (using air lock) in normal way. Rack off the lees when clear.

LOGANBERRY WINE

Ingredients:

1.3kg	**(3lb)**	**loganberries**
150ml		**grape concentrate**
1.3kg	**(3lb)**	**sugar**
		Yeast nutrient
		Pectic enzyme

Water to: 4.5 litres (1 gallon)

Method:

Wash the fruit in a colander gently so as not to damage it, losing juice. Either extract the juice by means of an extractor and add 2 litres (4 pints) boiling water, or put them in a bucket, pour on water, boiling, and mash the berries with a wooden spoon. Add 500g (1lb) sugar, stirring well to dissolve, and allow to cool to 70°F, then

"Heavenly bouquet."

introduce the yeast and yeast nutrient. Cover closely and leave for three days, stirring daily. Put the remaining 900g (2lb) sugar in a bowl, and strain the fermenting juice on to it; stir well to dissolve the sugar, then pour into an opaque or dark glass fermenting jar, and fit air lock. Top up if necessary (it should not be). Leave for three months, by which time it should be clearing. Rack off into a clean jar (again a dark one, to preserve the colour of the wine, which will go tawny if exposed to the light) and "top up" if necessary with boiled water or other red wine. Refit trap. Keep for another three months, then rack off again and bottle in dark bottles. A glorious, deep-red wine and the more fruit you use the more "body" it will have, but the bouquet is then likely to be too strong.

MADEIRA-TYPE WINE
4.5 litres (1 gallon)
(by P. Duncan and B. Acton)

Ingredients:

1.3kg	(3lb)	**plums or greengages**
570ml	(1 pint)	**white grape concentrate**
1kg	(2lb)	**bananas**
		Madeira yeast starter, yeast nutrients
		Tartaric acid and sugar as required
		Pectic enzyme

Method:

Stone the plums, peel and chop up the bananas (discarding the skins) and mix in the grape concentrate 450g (1lb) sugar. Pour about 3 litres (5 pints) boiling water over this mixture and when cool add the pectic enzyme, yeast nutrient and actively fermenting yeast starter. Ferment on the pulp for about 3-4 days, pushing down the cap of pulp at least twice daily, then strain off the fruit, removing as much pulp debris as possible.

Check the acidity and if necessary adjust to about 4.5 parts per thousand (in terms of sulphuric acid) by means of tartaric acid (probably one-third to two-thirds of an ounce according to the ripeness of the plums).

Make a syrup of 1kg (2lb) of sugar dissolved in 570ml (1 pint) of water. Add 280ml ($\frac{1}{2}$ pint) doses of sugar syrup whenever the gravity drops to five or below and continue feeding sugar in this way until the yeast reaches its maximum tolerance and fermentation ceases (this may take two to three months). The final volume should then be about 4.5 litres (one gallon).

After fermentation has ceased, rack the wine and place the jar in an "estufa" or hot cupboard, at 32-54°C (90-130°F) for three to twelve months according to temperature, racking every three months. Finally mature the wine at normal temperatures (around 13°C (55°F)) for at least one year, racking at six-month intervals. If a dry Sercial type wine is required, the adding of sugar dosages should be stopped when the fermentation is causing a gravity drop of only one or two points per day and providing there is at least 15 per cent alcohol in the wine.

MAIZE (see Barley)

MALMSEY-TYPE WINE
13.5 litres (3 gallons)
(by P. Duncan and B. Acton)

Ingredients:

450g	(1lb)	peach pulp
2kg	(4lb)	beetroot
1.3kg	(3lb)	bananas
		Madeira yeast starter, yeast nutrients
		Pectic enzyme
		Tartaric acid and sugar syrup as required

Method:

Wash the beet and cut into hunks, peel bananas and cut into slices, discarding the skins. Boil the beet and bananas in sufficient water to cover for $\frac{1}{2}$ hour and strain off the boiling liquor (noting the volume) over the peach pulp plus 1.25kg (2lb 11oz) sugar. Add enough cold water to make up to 9 litres (2 gallons) approximately. When cool add the yeast nutrients, pectic enzyme and actively fermenting yeast starter and ferment on the pulp for 2-3 days. Strain off the pulp, check acidity and adjust if necessary as in previous recipe and continue in the same way, feeding with 280ml doses of syrup and topping up the volume to three gallons eventually.

MINT WINE
(by C. S. Shave)

Ingredients:

800ml	(1½ pints)	mint leaves (lightly bruised)
280ml	(½ pint)	strong tea
1.3kg	(3lb)	sugar
		2 lemons or citric acid
		Yeast, yeast nutrient

Water to: 4.5 litres (1 gallon)

Method:

Dissolve the sugar in 3 litres (6 pints) boiling water and pour this over the mint leaves, add the strong tea, lemon juice or citric acid and lemon peel (no pith). Cool to 20°C (70°F) then stir in the yeast nutrient and an activated wine yeast, or 1 level teaspoon of granulated yeast. Ferment "on the solids" for 10 days, stirring each day, then strain and place in fermentation jar with fermentation lock, topping up if necessary and ferment in normal way.

Variations may be made by: (*a*) adding one pound chopped raisins and reducing sugar by 450g (1lb), or (*b*) adding 400ml grape concentrate and reducing sugar by one pound.

MULBERRY WINE

Ingredients:

1.8kg	(4lb)	mulberries
450g	(1lb)	raisins (dried figs, dates, prunes or apricots, etc, may be substituted)
55g	(2oz)	dried rose hips/shells (or 2oz dried bananas)
1.25kg	(2lb 11oz)	sugar

$\frac{1}{2}$oz citric acid (or 3 lemons, no pith, in lieu)
A pinch of grape tannin (or 280ml ($\frac{1}{2}$ pint) of strong tea)
Pectic enzyme
Yeast nutrient and activated wine yeast
Water to finally make up 4.5 litres (1 gallon) of must

Method:

Place the berries, chopped dried fruit, rose hips and sugar into the initial fermentation vessel. Pour in 3 litres (6 pints) boiling water. Macerate and stir well with a stainless steel or wooden spoon to break up the fruits and to dissolve the sugar. When cool add the citric acid, strong tea, pectic enzyme and yeast nutrient. Introduce the activated wine yeast and ferment "on the pulp" for 10 days, stirring the must twice daily, and keep it closely covered. Then strain, for secondary fermentation, into fermentation vessel top up with cold water, and fit air lock. Leave to ferment in the normal way, racking as necessary in due course.

"Red or white?
It doesn't matter;
I'm colour blind!"

OAKBUD WINE

Ingredients:

225g	($\frac{1}{2}$lb)	oak buds and young leaves
225g	($\frac{1}{2}$lb)	dates
225g	($\frac{1}{2}$lb)	raisins
1kg	(2.2lb)	sugar
		1 lemon
		Yeast and nutrient

Water to: 4.5 litres (1 gallon)

Method:

Gather the buds and new leaves as soon as the first leaves open. Bring 3.5 litres (6 pints) of water to the boil, then add the leaves, buds, and chopped dates and raisins, and simmer for 20 minutes. Strain the liquor on to the sugar and stir well to dissolve. Allow to cool to 20°C (70°F) then add the juice of the lemon, the yeast, and the yeast nutrient. Cover closely, and ferment in a warm place for four days before transferring to fermenting jar and fitting air lock. This is an excellent wine for blending purposes, for it will add zest to an insipid wine: if it is required sweet increase the sugar to 1.25kg (2lb 11oz) to produce a dry wine.

OAK LEAF WINE

Ingredients:

4 litres	(7 pints)	oak leaves
1.3kg	(3lb)	sugar
		2 oranges
		1 lemon
		Yeast and nutrient

Water to: 4.5 litres (1 gallon)

Method:

Young leaves will give a different flavour from those picked later in the year when they are brown-tinted, so here, really, are two wines.

Rinse the leaves in clean cold water, then place them in a polythene bucket and pour over them 3.5 litres (6 pints) of boiling water. Leave the leaves to steep for 24 hours, then strain the liquid into a boiler large enough to take both it and the sugar, with a little room to spare. Add the sugar, the juice of the fruit, and the grated peel, being careful to include no bitter white pith. Bring the whole to the boil and keep it simmering for 20 minutes. This serves the triple purpose of extracting the flavours and essences from the fruit skins, thoroughly dissolving the sugar, and sterilising the liquor. Allow to cool, strain again through a large nylon sieve or muslin, and when temperature has dropped to 20°C (70°F) add your chosen wine yeast or a level teaspoon of granulated yeast, pour into fermenting jar, and fit trap. This wine usually works vigorously, and will certainly do so if you include the yeast nutrient. You should have a little headspace in the fermenting bottle for the first four or five days, but after that top up with cold water, when the first vigour of the ferment has subsided. Otherwise it may foam out through the trap. When the wine has cleared (usually about two to three months) siphon off the yeast sediment and keep for at least six months before use.

Walnut leaf wine can be made in the same way.

"So much for encouraging junior to take up a hobby."

ONION WINE

Ingredients:

225g	($\frac{1}{4}$lb)	onions
225g	($\frac{1}{2}$lb)	potatoes
450g	(1lb)	chopped raisins
1.2kg	(2lb)	sugar
		2 lemons or citric acid
		Yeast nutrient
		Yeast (selected wine)

Water to: 4.5 litres (1 gallon)

Method:

Slice and dice the onions and potatoes and place these together with the chopped raisins in 3.5 litres (6 pints) of warm (not hot) water in which the sugar has been dissolved. Add lemon juice (no pith) or citric acid and yeast nutrient, then introduce activated yeast. Ferment for 10 days, then strain and complete fermentation in glass jars under fermentation lock.

ORANGE AND WHEAT

Ingredients:

		6 Jaffa oranges
450g	(1lb)	wheat
100g	($\frac{1}{4}$lb)	raisins
		1 lemon
1.2kg	(2lb 11oz)	sugar
		Yeast; nutrient

Water to: 4.5 litres (1 gallon)

Method:

Bring 3.5 litres (6 pints) of water to the boil, then simmer the skins of the citrus fruit in it for a quarter of an hour. Take out the peel and pour the liquid over the sugar, the juice of the oranges and lemons, the washed wheat, and the chopped raisins. Allow to cool to 20°C (70°F) before adding the yeast and yeast nutrient, and keep well covered in a warm place, stirring daily, for 10 days. Then strain into fermenting jar, and top up if necessary (the grain absorbs some of the liquid). Fit trap, and ferment out, rack and bottle in the usual way.

SEVILLE ORANGE WINE

Ingredients:

		6 Seville oranges
		6 sweet oranges
1kg	**(2lb 4oz)**	**sugar (for a dry wine)**
1.2kg	**(2lb 11oz)**	**sugar (for a sweet wine)**
		Yeast; nutrient

Water to: 4.5 litres (1 gallon)

Method:

Wash the oranges in warm water to remove any wax and peel three of each, keeping the peel thin and avoiding the pith, which imparts a very bitter flavour. Boil 3 litres ($5\frac{1}{4}$ pints) of water and then add the peel to it; cover, and allow to stand for 24 hours to extract the zest. Then strain the infusion into a polythene bucket containing the sugar, and the juice of all twelve oranges. Stir until all the sugar is dissolved, and then add the yeast and yeast nutrient. Cover the bucket closely and stand in a warm place 20°C (70°F) for four or five days, after which the ferment will have quietened a little and the liquor can be poured into a fermenting jar and a trap fitted. Leave until it clears, then rack and bottle as usual.

SWEET ORANGE WINE

Ingredients:

		12 sweet oranges
		1 lemon
1.3kg	(3lb)	sugar
450g	(1lb)	large raisins
		Yeast; nutrient

Water to: 4.5 litres (1 gallon)

Method:

Peel half the oranges and put the skins in the oven, baking them until they are browned; then pour over them 1 litre (2 pints) of water, boiling. Peel the remaining oranges, and then pulp all the oranges in a polythene bucket. Add the chopped or minced raisins and the Campden tablet, and pour over the fruit 2 litres (3 pints 10oz) of water, cold, and the liquid from the orange-peel infusion. Stir well, cover closely, and leave for 24 hours. Add the lemon juice, yeast, nutrient, and 450g (1lb) sugar, stirring well to dissolve. Stir the must daily and keep in a warm place 20°C (70°F). After four days strain on to remaining sugar, stirring well to dissolve, and pour into fermenting jar. Fit trap, and ferment at roughly 18°C (65°F) until clear; then rack. Keep a further two months under air lock before bottling.

PARSLEY AND RICE

(by Humfrey Wakefield)

Ingredients:

225g	($\frac{1}{2}$lb)	raisins
1 litre	(1 quart)	measure parsley (packed tight)
100g	($\frac{1}{4}$lb)	rice
1kg	(2-2$\frac{1}{4}$lb)	sugar
		Grated rind of 2 oranges
		Grated rind and juice of 1 lemon
		Nutrient
		Tokay yeast
		Pectic enzyme, as instructed

Method:

Boil parsley (well washed) in 2 litres ($\frac{1}{2}$ gallon) of water. Put in rice and simmer further five minutes. Strain through coarse sieve on to sugar, grated rinds, lemon juice and coarsely chopped raisins. Sir well. When cool, add yeast (previously propagated in a starter bottle), and Pectasin (or Amylozyme) dissolved in a little warm water.

Add water (about 2 litres) to bring bulk of must up to near 4.5 litres (1 gallon).

Ferment on raisin-pulp for 2-4 days, stirring frequently, and keeping covered.

Strain off into gallon jar through coarse sieve, and top up (if necessary) with water. Fit lock. Rack when wine begins to clear, and again when fermentation is quite finished.

Produces a light, fragrant white table wine, something between pineapple and apricot. Don't worry about chickenbroth smell in early stages. It ferments out. If sweet dessert wine is wanted (also good), add a further 450g (1lb) sugar when fermentation begins to slow.

"We hate small glasses."

PARSNIP WINE

Ingredients:

1.8kg	(4lb)	parsnips
1.25kg	(2lb 11oz)	sugar
150ml		grape concentrate
15g		citric acid
		Pectinol or Pektolase, as directed

Water to: 4.5 litres (1 gallon)

Method:

Scrub the parsnips and scrape them quickly with a strong knife, then slice them and boil them in 3.5 litres (6 pints) of water until just tender, but on no account so long that they go mushy, or the wine will not clear. If the roots are boiled in half the water, for convenience sake, the remainder can be added later.

Strain through a large nylon sieve on to the remaining water (cold) but do not press the parsnips or hurry the process unduly, or again, the wine may not clear. Add the sugar and concentrate, bring to the boil and then turn down the heat and simmer gently for three-quarters of an hour. Turn into a crock or pan, and allow to cool to 20°C (70°F); then add Pectic enzyme, citric acid, yeast and yeast nutrient, preferably a wine yeast, but a level teaspoon of granulated yeast can be employed failing anything better. Cover closely with a thick cloth, and keep in a warm place for a week 17°-20°C (60°-70°F). Then pour into fermenting jar, top up and fit air lock. Rack when it clears, and refit air lock, and rack for the second time after a further three months.

PARSNIP WINE (Spiced)

Ingredients:

2.5kg	(6lb)	parsnips
1kg	(2lb 11oz)	sugar
		1 lemon
		2 oranges
30g	(1oz)	root ginger
		Yeast; yeast nutrient
		Pectic enzyme

Water to: 4.5 litres (1 gallon)

Method:

Midwinter is the time to make this wine, for the sugar content of the roots will have been concentrated by the winter frosts. Scrape or scrub the parsnips clean (a strong-bladed, large knife is a great help), slice them, and boil in 3.5 litres (6 pints) of water until tender, but not mushy. (Be careful not to overdo the boiling or you will subsequently have difficulty clearing the wine. If you have a press you need boil for only 5-10 minutes, for you can then press the parsnips afterwards.) The bruised ginger and the thinly-pared rinds of the citrus fruit are boiled in with the parsnips (or separately, in a litre or so of the water if you are using the press; this is then added to the remainder). Strain all the liquid on to the juice of the fruit and dissolve the sugar in it, stirring well. Cool to 20°C (70°F), then add the yeast and yeast nutrient and the Pectic enzyme, and cover. Stir daily. Four of five days later, stir, and pour into fermenting jar, and fit trap. Leave in a warm place to ferment until the wine clears and a yeast deposit has formed (about two months) and then rack for the first time. Refit trap and leave until completely clear and stable (another two months or so) then rack again and bottle.

Grape? Haven't you got any PROPER wine?

PARSNIP AND BANANA
(see under Banana)

PARSNIP AND FIG

Ingredients:

1.3kg	(3lb)	parsnips
500g	(1lb)	dried figs
225g	(¼lb)	raisins
225g	(½lb)	rice
1.25kg	(2lb 11oz)	sugar
		Yeast and yeast nutrient
		Pectic enzyme

Water to: 4.5 litres (1 gallon)

Method:

Scrub or scrape the parsnips, slice them, and boil them in half the water with the chopped figs and raisins until only just tender, usually not more than 20 minutes. Do not "over-cook" so that the parsnips go soft and mushy, or the wine may subsequently be difficult to clear. Then strain the liquor on to the rice, bring to the boil, and boil for four minutes. Strain on to the sugar and stir well to dissolve. Allow the liquor to cool to 20°C (70°F) then add the Pectic enzyme, yeast – a sherry yeast is excellent – and yeast nutrient, and pour into a fermenting jar or bottle. Fill to shoulder adding cold boiled water if necessary, and fit an air lock. After about a week in a temperature of 17°-20°C (65°-70°F) the first vigorous ferment will have subsided and the jar can be topped up to the bottom of the neck. When the wine begins to clear and a yeast deposit has formed (six weeks to two months) siphon it off the lees into a fresh bottle and refit lock. Leave for a further three months before bottling. This will usually produce a dry wine if a good nutrient has been used, and some readers may care to add 4-8ozs more sugar either before fermentation ceases or to the finished wine.

PARSNIP AND BEETROOT
(See under Beetroot and Parnsip)

PEACH PERFECTION

This is a recipe by Mrs Cherry Leeds, of Thames Ditton, for a peach wine which is so superb — and *cheap* — that we give the fullest possible instructions ...

It sounds extravagant, but it is not. Keep an eye on the greengrocer's and you'll see that in August (usually about the first fortnight) peaches come right down in price, to 9p each or even less. The wine works out at about 10p a bottle.

Mrs Leeds uses a Kitzinger sherry or Tokay yeast, and here we give again her recipes, for the benefit of the many readers who have requested them:

TO MAKE 10 GALLONS

Ingredients:

13kg	(30lb)	peaches
14kg	(32lb)	sugar (10 Demerara)
		Boiling and boiled water
85g	(3oz)	citric acid
		1½ teaspoons tannin
85g	(3oz)	Pectic enzyme

Method:

Wipe peaches and remove the stones; drop into large container such as a polythene bin. Scrub hands well and squeeze the peaches until well mashed. Well cover with boiling water and leave covered overnight.

The next day stir in the Pectic enzyme and cover well. On the third day strain through a sieve or muslin, twice if possble to reduce sludge, and put into the 10-gallon jar; add citric acid, tannin and nutrient.

At this point it is a simple matter to place the jar or carboy into the position it will occupy during fermentation. Put 9kg (20lb) of sugar into the large container and add sufficient boiling water to dissolve, and when cool add to the jar. Then the level of the liquid is brought up to the turn of the shoulder of the jar with boiled water. Open the yeast sachet or packet, pour in, and fit fermentation lock. The gravity at this stage will be about 100; the original gravity is almost invariably 25-30. Fermentation will start on the third day if the temperature is sufficient 20-25°C (70°-75°F).

The rest of the sugar is added in stages from now on, the first addition of 2 litres (4 pints) of syrup when the gravity is 30, that is, roughly, after two weeks. The sugar is then added in 1 litre (2 pint) lots when the gravity is between 10 and 15 each time. The syrup used is 1kg (2.2lb) sugar to 570m (1 pint) boiling water and cooled, thus making 1.1 litres (2 pints) syrup.

The fermenting period lasts for about seven or eight months, though one can keep it going for a year with small additions of syrup.

The first racking takes place when all the sugar is in and the reading is 10. Some of the wine will have to be removed to accommodate the last litre (2 pints) of syrup. Stir up the jar and remove about a litre. Put it by, under an air lock, and this can be used to top up the jar after the first racking. Stir the liquid vigorously with an oak rod once a day for the first few weeks.

Because of the pectic enzyme used the wine will clear perfectly and after the first racking will become crystal clear, but don't be tempted to rack again until fermentation has ceased finally. This usually happens when the gravity is about five.

The alcoholic content will be about 18%.

TO MAKE FIVE GALLONS

For 25 litre (5 gallon) jars use half quantities exept for the pectic enzyme – this is 55g (20z) – otherwise the procedure is the same.

TO MAKE ONE GALLON
Ingredients:

1.3kg	(3lb)	peaches
		1 teaspoon citric acid
15g	($\frac{1}{2}$oz)	pectic enzyme
		saltspoon tannin
1kg	(2.2lb)	sugar
2.25 litres	($\frac{1}{2}$ gallon)	boiling water

Method:

The method is the same but the yeast starter bottle is prepared on the same day as mashing, and the sugar is put in all together, just before the yeast starter.

PINEAPPLE AND BEET
(see under Beet and Pineapple)

PLUM WINE (1)

Ingredients:

1.8kg	**(4lb)**	**plums**
1.3kg	**(3lb)**	**white sugar**
		Yeast and yeast nutrient
		Pectic enzyme

Water to: 4.5 litres (1 gallon)

Method:

Wash the fruit and cut it up, then put it in a bowl and pour over it 3 litres of water, boiling. Cover it with a thick cloth or sheet of polythene, and when it is cool add the pectic enzyme, according to

"Rail crash? No, just the Winemakers Circle committee meeting...."

maker's instructions. Leave four days, giving it an occasional stir. Then strain through a nylon sieve or muslin, dissolve sugar in the juice, and add yeast. Cover again, and two days later pour into fermenting jar and fit trap. Top up to bottom of neck with cold water. When the wine clears siphon off the lees, keep for a further three months, then rack into bottles. More fruit can be used if available to lend more body to the wine, or, failing that, 500g (1lb) of wheat or barley (plum wine does tend to be rather thin).

PLUM WINE (2)

Ingredients:

1.8kg	**(4lb)**	**plums**
		1 lemon
1.2kg	**(2lb 11oz)**	**sugar**
		4 cloves
10g	**($\frac{1}{4}$oz)**	**root ginger**
		Yeast and nutrient
		Pectic enzyme

Water to: 4.5 litres (1 gallon)

Method:

This is basically a very old recipe, from the days when additional flavourings were favoured, and to our mind the cloves and ginger are just as well omitted, but we give the entire recipe for those who like the old fashioned wines.

Cut up the plums, removing the stones, and add to them the crushed ginger, the cloves, and the sliced lemon. Bring 3 litres of water to the boil and pour it over these ingredients, and stir. When it cools add the pectic enzyme. Cover and leave for three or four days, stirring twice daily. Strain through a fine sieve on to the sugar, stir to dissolve it, and add the yeast and nutrient. Put into fermenting jar, top up with water to bottom of neck, and fit trap; leave to ferment to a finish in a warm place. When clear and stable siphon off into clean bottles and cork.

CHERRY PLUM WINE

by Mrs Dorothy Cuthbertson (Liverpool Guild)

The Liverpool Guild were so impressed by this cheap-to-make wine (cheap when cherry plums are in season) that they suggested Mrs Cuthbertson have the recipe published. It makes, she says, a wine very similar to a Sauternes. Here it is:

Ingredients:

1.8kg	**(4lb)**	**cherry plums**
450g	**(1lb)**	**raisins (chopped)**
		2 teaspoons citric acid
1.2kg	**(2lb 11oz)**	**sugar (according to taste)**
		¼ teacup of strong tea
		All-purpose wine yeast
		Yeast nutrient
		Pectic enzyme

"Just a shade too effervescent!"

Method:

Wash fruit, cover with 3 litres (5 pints 5oz) boiling water, add 2lb sugar, tea, raisins, citric acid; when cool add pectic enzyme, yeast starter and yeast food. Stir and squeeze the fruit daily for five days, then strain into fermentation jar and fit lock. Add sugar in syrup form as required. (Not more than 450g dissolved in 250ml of water.)

Keep the fermentation going as long as possible, but when it finally ceases and the wine is clear and stable siphon into clean bottles.

PORT-TYPE WINE

(by P. Duncan and B. Acton)

Ingredients:

1.3kg	(3lb)	elderberries
900g	(2lb)	bananas
570ml	(1 pint)	red grape concentrate
		Tartaric acid, nutrient, sugar syrup as required
		Port yeast

Method:

Mash elderberries to extract juice, and leach pulp with 570ml (1 pint) cold water. Boil bananas in 1 litre (2 pints) water and add liquor to elderberry juice plus leachings and grape concentrate. Bring volume up to 4 litres (7 pints) and adjust acid to between 3.5 and 4.0 parts per thousands as sulphuric acid (this requires the addition of 15g ($\frac{1}{2}$oz) tartaric acid). Add yeast nutrient when cool and a good port yeast culture, and feed with additions of syrup in quarter-pint lots (syrup made with 2lb sugar in 1 pint of water) whenever the wine tastes dry (or drops in gravity to 5). When fermentation is almost finished, rack and top up to 4.5 litres (1 gallon) with water and syrup so that the final gravity is around 10. This, for those who do not use a hydrometer, would mean adding a final 150ml (quarter-pint) of syrup, or a little more.

In view of the relatively high cost of this wine, it will be worth keeping for at least two years, and preferably three, racking at three-month intervals in order that the maximum flavour and smoothness may develop.

An equally satisfactory Port-type wine can be made by using 1.3kg (3lb) blackberries, 900g (2lb) sloes or damsons, and 450g (1lb) elderberries, mashing and leaching these and then proceeding as above.

For a tawny wine, use 2.7kg (6lb) blackberries only and keep finished wine for three or four years.

PRUNE WINE
(by H E Bravery)

Ingredients:
**1.8kg   (4lb)   prunes
           2 lemons
1.2kg   (2lb 11oz) sugar
           Yeast and nutrient
           Pectic enzyme**
Water to: 4.5 litres (1 gallon)

Method:

Wash the prunes in water and put them in the fermenting vessel. Boil 800g (1¾lb) of sugar in 3 litres (5 pints 5oz) of water and pour over the fruit while boiling. Allow to cool and add the yeast and pectic enzyme. Cover and ferment for 10 days, crushing well each day as soon as the fruit has become soft.

After 10 days, crush well and strain out the solids. Wring out as dry as you can and put the strained liquor into a gallon jar.

Boil the remaining 400g of sugar in 280ml. (½ pint) of water and when cool add to the rest. Top up with a little cold water if necessary. Cover or fit fermentation lock and leave until all fermentation has ceased. Then rack and bottle as usual.

PRUNE AND BANANA
(see under Banana)

PRUNE AND WHEAT WINE
(by Syd Lowe)

Ingredients:

450g	**(1lb)**	**prunes (best quality)**
450g	**(1lb)**	**wheat (best quality)**
100g	**(¼lb)**	**raisins**
1kg	**(2.2lb)**	**sugar**
		1 Yeast nutrient tablet
		Pectic enzyme
		2 Vitamin B tablets
		(Aneurine hydrochloride BP)
		Yeast, sherry yeast (or 1 level teaspoon dried yeast)

Water to: 4.5 litres (1 gallon)

Method:

Cut each prune through with a knife into a bucket. Place wheat in a moderate oven to lightly bake (do not allow to brown over), then add to prunes, with yeast nutrient, raisins, pectic enzyme (as makers direct) and Vitamin B. Pour on 3.5 litres (6 pints) of water that has been boiled and allowed to cool, cover, and stir very thoroughly every day for 10 days. Strain and press pulp to extract all the juice. (Do this with your hands if no other means available.) Add 800g (1¾lb) sugar made into syrup with a small amount of warm water. Add yeast, stir thoroughly to mix.

Leave this in a warm place for about 10 days, then strain through muslin or jelly bag into gallon jar and fit air lock. After it has been in the jar for about 10 days, sample it and, if necessary, add a little of the 450g (1lb) of sugar that you have left. Repeat this after another 10 days; then add the balance. Top up with cold water if necessary.

Leave until fermentation is complete. Strain into clean jar, fit cork, and leave in cool place (a cellar is ideal) until it clears perfectly; then bottle.

PUMPKIN WINE

Ingredients:

1.8kg	**(4lb)**	**pumpkin**
1.2kg	**(2lb 11oz)**	**white sugar**
		2 lemons
		1oz of root ginger (this can be omitted if desired)
		2 oranges
		Yeast and nutrient

Water to: 4.5 litres (1 gallon)

Method:

Grate the pumpkin, slice the oranges and lemons, bruise the ginger and put them all into a polythene bucket. Pour over them 3.5 litres (6 pints) of boiling water and when cool add the yeast and nutrient. Allow to stand for five days closely covered, stirring frequently, then strain and dissolve the sugar in the liquid. After four or five days' fermentation, closely covered, put it into a fermentation jar and fit trap. When it clears siphon off the yeast. The pumpkin wine should be ready after about six months and then can be bottled.

RED CURRANT WINE (1)

This is a popular wine and well worth making, but often tends to turn out disappointingly "thin" for those who prefer good body in their wines. If you require a delicate wine, make it according to the recipe, but if you want a slightly heavier wine, use additional fruit, 200g (about ½lb) of rolled barley (most mills can supply it) and pour the water on boiling instead of cold. In that case omit the pectic enzyme and Campden tablet.

Ingredients:

1.3kg	(3lb)	**red currants**
1.3kg	(3lb)	**sugar**
		Pectic enzyme
		Yeast and nutrient

Water to: 4.5 litres (1 gallon)

Method:

Put the fruit in a polythene bucket and crush thoroughly, then add 2 litres (4 pints) of cold water and one crushed Campden tablet. 24 hours later add the pectic enzyme according to the makers' instructions. Cover closely and leave for five or six days, stirring daily. Then strain through a nylon sieve or jellybag, expressing as much juice as possible, into a fermenting vessel. Add the sugar, stirring well to dissolve it, yeast and nutrient, fit a fermentation lock, and leave in a temperature of about 20°C (70°F) to ferment. Top up a week later (if at all necessary with cold water). Rack the wine off the lees when it clears, refit the air lock, and repeat the process about three months later, when it will probably be stable and ready to bottle. Again, dark bottles will preserve its delicate colour.

RED CURRANT WINE (2)

Ingredients:

1.8 kilo	**4lb**	**red currants**
4 litres	**7 pints**	**water**
1.5 kilo	**3½lb**	**sugar**
		Yeast and nutrient

Method:

As for cherry (1) or blackcurrant.

About oxalic acid

Many older winemaking books lay undue emphasis upon the presence in rhubarb of oxalic acid, which is poisonous, and on the need to remove it. The oxalic acid, however, is contained in the leaves of the plant, and not in the stalks, which we winemakers use.

Rhubarb is unduly acid, however, and it may well be advisable to reduce the natural acid a little and/or use some citric acid in a recipe.

Acid can be removed before fermentation by stirring in 1oz per gallon (30g per 4.5 litres) of precipitated chalk, or powdered cuttlefish. The juice will effervesce. If afterwards it still has an acid taste add up to another 15g (½oz) but not more. Finally, to give you the acidity you need, add the juice of three lemons, or one heaped teaspoon of citric acid. A little more may be necessary; taste the juice, adjust to taste or by testing with a titration kit.

RHUBARB (1) "GOLDEN DREAM"

Ingredients:

2.5kg	(6lb)	red rhubarb
450g	(1lb)	malt extract
1.8kg	(4lb)	white sugar
		Pinch of grape tannin
		2 lemons (or 1 teaspoon citric acid)
		Yeast (selected wine)

Method:

Whether or not any acid should be removed by precipitated chalk is a matter of opinion, I have made it with or without! The rhubarb stalks should be picked in mid-May and malt extract is used to add body to the wine.

Do not peel the rhubarb but wipe the stalks clean, cut into small short lengths and cover with cold or warm (not boiling) water and soak for three days, crushing the rhubarb with the hands after the second day. Then strain off into fermenting vessel. Dissolve sugar and malt extract, adding this with tannin and lemon juice, or one teaspoon of citric acid, to the strained rhubarb juice. Add yeast nutrient and an activated wine yeast and ferment in the normal way.

An often repeated recipe for a favourite "golden" wine.

RHUBARB (2)
MEMORABLE NECTAR

Ingredients:

2.5kg	**(6lb)**	**red rhubarb, picked mid-May**
450g	**(1lb)**	**raisins**
280ml	**½ pint**	**strong tea or a little grape tannin**
		Yeast nutrient and yeast (selected wine)
1.5kg	**(3½lb)**	**sugar**
		2 lemons or 1 teaspoon citric acid

Method:

Prepare rhubarb juice as in "Golden Dream". The raisins should be cut up and simmered in the strong tea and the pulp strained into the rhubarb juice. After dissolving the sugar and adding the lemon juice and/or citric acid to the juice add the yeast nutrient and a working wine yeast; ferment in the normal way.

Very popular in the Midlands, and another of my favourites.

"Some of these old recipes use large quantities. . . "

RHUBARB (3)
GOLDEN PIPKIN
(by C. Shave)

Ingredients:

1.3kg	(3lb)	red rhubarb
200ml	($\frac{1}{4}$ pint)	strong tea
1kg	(2lb 11oz)	sugar
200ml	($\frac{1}{4}$ pint)	grape concentrate (white)
		2 lemons or 1 teaspoon citric acid
		Yeast nutrient
		Yeast (selected wine)

Method:

Prepare as "Golden Dream", substituting the grape concentrate for the malt extract, giving a much lighter and finer wine.

"CHRISTMAS PORT"

Having made in May either "Golden Dream" or "Memorable Nectar" and given it its first racking it will be blackberry time.

Pick 1.3kg (3lb) blackberries and cover them with 570ml (1 pint) boiling water, adding 110g ($\frac{1}{4}$lb) sugar, then squeeze pulp through muslin and add the juice to the racked rhubarb wine. Fit fermentation lock and ferment on in the usual way. A most satisfying wine.

"WINTER CHEER"

Ingredients:

2.5kg	(6lb)	red rhubarb (picked mid-May)
1 litre	(1 quart)	balm leaves or 1 packet dried leaves
1.8kg	(4lb)	sugar
		2 lemons or 1 teaspoon citric acid
		Yeast nutrient
		Yeast (selected wine)
280ml	($\frac{1}{2}$ pint)	strong tea, or $\frac{1}{8}$ teaspoon grape tannin

Method:

Prepare rhubarb juice as in "Golden Dream". Put balm leaves in saucepan with water and bring to boil with lemon peel (no pith), cutting off heat as soon as water is boiling. Allow to stand for 15 minutes, strain and add this to rhubarb juice, pouring over dissolved sugar, lemon juice or citric acid and strong tea. Add yeast nutrient and a selected wine yeast started fermenting in normal way.

"Winter Cheer" may be varied by the addition of 450g (1lb) of malt extract to the gallon, giving more body, or 450g (1lb) of raisins for eventually that grand old-time mellow flavour.

RICE WINE
(Wheat, or rye, can be substituted if desired)

Ingredients:

To make two gallons:

225g	**(8oz)**	**rice (wheat, rye)**
3kg	**(7lb)**	**sugar**
9 litres	**(2 gallons)**	**water**
10g	**($\frac{1}{3}$oz)**	**citric acid**
		1pkt Vierka sherry yeast
		1pkt Vierka nutrient salt
		1 Campden tablet

Water to: 9 litres (2 gallons)

"...but I only drink a gallon of it a day..."

Method:

Two or three days in advance prepare a starter for the yeast by bringing 570ml (1 pint) apple juice to the boil with a pinch of nutrient salt and a tablespoon of sugar. Add yeast and leave, plugged with cotton wool, in a temperature of 20° (70°F).

On the third day after starting the yeast, boil 225g (8oz) rice in 3 litres (5 pints) water with the addition of two tablespoonfuls sugar, for five minutes only. Allow to cool, and add the yeast starter, now in full ferment, together with the one teaspoon nutrient salt, and citric acid (about three level teaspoonsful).

By the next day the rice-pulp is in vigorous fermentation. Add what remains of the sugar 3kg (7lb) (less three tablespoons) dissolved in the rest of the water 9 litres (2 gallons) less 3 litres (5 pints), and pour into a clean fermenting jar. Strain the fermenting pulp on to the syrup (when cool), through a clean linen bag or handkerchief, with the help of a funnel. Press out lightly with the hands, so that some of the rice-starch goes into the jar.

Don't fill to the brim yet, but leave room for foaming. If need be keep back some of the syrup till the tumultuous ferment has died down, say after 14 days.

The wine will take about two months to ferment right out. Then is the time for the first racking. Top up with pure water, and allow a further four weeks in the warm for the secondary fermentation. Rack again, lightly sulphite with the Campden tablet, and put in the cool for another four weeks.

The wine will then be as clear as water, and can be coloured lightly with edible colouring matter, or blackcurrant juice, before drawing off into bottles.

RICE WINE (Chinese)

Ingredients:

1.3kg	(3lb)	paddy rice (polished rice will not do)
1.3kg	(3lb)	honey
4.5 litres	(1 gallon)	water
		the juice of 2 lemons, 2 oranges
		(These quantities are the suggested ones; precise amounts were not given in the original Chinese recipe.)

Method:

"Steep the grain for 20 days in water, stirring every day, and keeping well covered. Bring it to the boil and boil it gently until the grains are soft and pulpy, then put it into an earthenware crock (with your gallon of water). To the must are then added various fruits and flowers, and a percentage of honey to give strength, aroma and colour to the wine.

"In China whence comes this recipe, lemon or lime flowers are added according to the taste of the maker, the juice of oranges or lemons, and the thinly peeled rinds.

"When the must is all well blended and has cooled yeast is added and it is allowed to ferment in a jar for several days. The wine is then strained into clean, glazed vessels, where by a second ferment it clears itself. When the ferment in the second jar is finished, the wine is drawn off into small earthenware jars which are sealed down and set aside to mature. Well made, this wine is very strong in alcohol content and will keep for many years. It can be distilled (but not in this country!) into the Chinese spirit called Sam Choo."

RICE WINE
(Old English version)

Steep 3lb of paddy rice, in half a gallon of water for six days, stirring every day. Then put into another bowl 3lb of sugar, the juice and rind of two or three lemons and oranges, and, if liked, a few spices. Pour a gallon of boiling water on to the fruit and sugar and stir until it is all blended; then strain the water from the rice and add it to the mixture. When the liquor has cooled to about 70°F add yeast, cover the bowl and leave for 24 hours. Then strain carefully into a cask and leave in a warm place to finish the ferment. Top up each morning with water and drop in a stoned raisin each day when the fermentation begins to flag. When all movement has ceased, bung down the cask and store for a year.

RICE AND BANANA
(see under Banana)

RICE AND PARSLEY
(see Parsley and Rice)

RICE
(see Barley)

ROSEHIP WINE

Ingredients:

1.4kg	(3lb)	rosehips
1kg	(2.2lb)	white sugar
		Yeast; yeast nutrient

Water to: 4.5 litres (1 gallon)

Method:

Wash your rosehips thoroughly in a colander, and then either cut them in half or crush them with a piece of wood. A good way of tackling this rather tricky job is to use a domestic mincer with the outer cutting disc removed. Use the fixed disc with the largest holes and this will just neatly crush the pips. To do so by hand with a mallet or roller is rather a sticky and messy business! Put the crushed rosehips and sugar into a crock or polythene dustbin and pour over them 3.5 litres (6 pints) of boiling water; stir well until the sugar is completely dissolved.

Allow the liquor to cool to about 20°C (70°F) (cool enough for you to be able to put your finger in it comfortably) and add your yeast, an all-purpose wine yeast or, failing that, a level teaspoon of granulated yeast, together with some yeast nutrient. Cover the container closely with a thick cloth or polythene and leave in a warm place for a fortnight, stirring daily.

Then strain through a nylon sieve or two thicknesses of butter muslin into a fermentation jar, and fit an air lock. This wine usually ferments very vigorously, and will normally clear after about three months. Siphon it into a fresh jar, not disturbing the sediment, and leave for a further three months before bottling.

ROSEHIP (Dried)

Ingredients:

300g	**(12oz)**	**dried rosehips**
1kg	**(2.2lb)**	**sugar**
		juice of 1 lemon
		Tokaier yeast and yeast nutrient

Water to: 4.5 litres (1 gallon)

Method:

Dried rosehips can be purchased and one can thus avoid the tedious business of picking fresh hips. The dried ones make a wine fully as good, and rosehip wine *is* good, indeed the Germans hold that it is second only to the grape for winemaking. With the dried rosehips, which have been largely dehydrated, and therefore weigh less, a smaller quantity is required than when one uses the fresh fruit.

Prepare your yeast starter two days before making the wine and soak the rosehips overnight in 500ml (1 pint) of water.

Mince your rosehips through an ordinary domestic mincer with the outer cutting disc removed and put into a bowl with the sugar and lemon juice. Pour over them 3 litres (5 pints 5oz) of water, boiling. Stir well to dissolve the sugar. When the mixture has cooled to 20°C (70°F) add your fermenting Tokaier yeast. Cover closely with a polythene sheet secured by elastic and stand in a warm place (about 70°F) but stir daily. After 10 days, strain into a 4.5 litre (1 gallon) jar, topping up with cold boiling water to the bottom of the neck (if necessary) and fit fermentation lock. When the wine clears rack into a clean jar and refit lock. Leave for a further three months, then rack into clean bottles and cork down.

ROSEHIP SHELL AND FIG

Ingredients:

150g	(6oz)	dried rosehip shells
100g	(4oz)	dried figs
1.25kg	(2lb 11oz)	sugar (1kg for a dry wine)
		Tokaier yeast

Method:

Put the figs in just enough water to cover them and leave overnight. The next day add a little more water, bring to the boil, and simmer for 10 minutes. Strain the juice into a saucepan and make quantity up to 3.5 litres (6 pints). Bring to the boil and pour over the rosehip shells, sugar and lemon juice. Stir well to dissolve sugar. Allow to cool to 20°C (70°F) and then add your yeast. Cover closely with a polythene sheet secured by elastic and stand in a warm place (about 20°C) for 10 days, stirring daily. Then strain into fermenting jar and fit air lock. Ferment until the wine clears and fermentation slows, then rack into a clean jar, and refit lock. Rack again after three months into clean bottles, and cork down.

ROSEHIP AND DRIED BANANA
(see under Banana)

ROSEHIP SHELL AND BANANA
(see under Banana)

ROSEHIP SYRUP

Rosehip syrup provides an easy way of making wine and a 170ml (6oz) bottle is sufficient to make 4.5 litres (1 gallon). Brands commonly available are Delrosa (in 170ml and 340ml – 6fl oz and 12fl oz – sizes) and Optrose (170ml – 6fl oz). Boots do a very dark red in 200ml (7.04fl oz) and 350ml (12.3fl oz) sizes, and a pink syrup "free of added colour" in the same sizes.

"I don't think it really matters HOW you serve wine, do you?"

You can also buy blackcurrant and rosehip, and orange and rosehip, which can be used for winemaking in exactly the same way as straight rosehip syrup.

Ingredients:

170ml	(1 small bottle)	rosehip syrup
1kg	(2.2lb)	sugar
3.5 litres	(6 pints)	water
10g	($\frac{1}{4}$oz)	citric acid
		Yeast and nutrient

Method:

Merely bring the water to the boil, add the syrup and sugar, and stir well to dissolve. When cool 20°C, (70°F) add the citric acid, yeast and nutrient, and stir again. Pour into fermenting jar and fit airlock, leaving in a warm place to ferment. After a week or so top up to bottom of neck with cold boiled water and refit lock. Ferment, rack and bottle in usual way.

ROSEMARY WINE

(Rosmarinus officinalis)

"There's rosemary, that's for remembrance." SHAKESPEARE.

Ingredients:

		1 small packet Rosemary Herb
15g	($\frac{1}{2}$oz)	citric acid (or 3 lemons, no pith, in lieu)
1.3kg	(3lb)	sugar
		A pinch of grape tannin
150ml	($\frac{1}{4}$ pint)	grape concentrate
		Yeast nutrient and activated wine yeast

Water to: 4.5 litres (1 gallon)

Method:

Pour 2.5 litres (6 pints) of boiling water over the Rosemary Herb and infuse as for tea. Strain on to sugar and stir to dissolve sugar. When cool add the grape tannin, citric acid and grape concentrate. Then when cool add the yeast nutrient and activated wine yeast. Fit air lock to fermenting vessel and leave until it clears. Rack and bottle in due course, 3/4 months later.

SARSAPARILLA AND BANANA

(see under Banana)

SAUTERNES

(by P. Duncan and B. Acton)

Ingredients:

900g	(2lb)	bananas
1.3kg	(3lb)	ripe gooseberries or apricots (or tin of Apricot Pulp)
500ml	(1 pint)	white grape concentrate
280ml	(½ pint)	elderflowers or a packet of dried flowers
30ml	(1fl oz)	glycerol (obtained at any chemist as glycerine)
		Yeast nutrient
5g	(1/10oz)	tannin
		Sauternes yeast
		Sugar syrup as required, made by boiling 2lb sugar with 1 pint water (900g in 570ml)
		Acid as required to produce acidity 5.2 p.p.t. sulphur; or if not using acid testing kit, between 10 and 25g (¼oz and ¾oz) acid (equal parts malic acid and tartaric acid or a citric/malic/tartaric mixture). Riper fruit will require the addition of more acid than less ripe fruit.

Water to: 4.5 litres (1 gallon)

Method:

Peel bananas and boil (with skins) in 1 litre (2 pints) of water for half an hour. Put concentrate, fruit and flowers in a plastic bucket and strain boiling liquor from bananas over them. When cool bring liquid content up to 3.5 litres (six pints) by adding about 800ml cold water. Add 10g (¼oz) citric acid, tannin, glycerol and nutrient and then a vigorously fermenting Sauternes yeast starter. After three days strain off fruit and continue fermentation in a fermenting jar or other container closed with an air lock adding 150ml (¼ pint) doses of sugar syrup whenever wine goes dry (or gravity drops to below 10). If fermentation proceeds longer than eight weeks, make a preliminary racking with plenty of splashing to aerate the wine and add further nutrients to continue fermentation to its final point. When fermentation ceases, rack and sulphite 100 parts per million (two Campden tablets per 4.5 litres (1 gallon)). Mature for at least a year, preferably in cask, racking at three-monthly intervals and sulphiting each time (50 p.p., or 1 Campden tablet).

SHERRY

(Dry Fino type)
(by P. Duncan and B. Acton)

Ingredients:

450g	(1lb)	bananas
570ml	(1 pint)	white grape concentrate
15g	($\frac{1}{2}$oz)	tartaric acid
30g	(1oz)	gypsum (calcium sulphate)
		Yeast nutrient
		Sugar to be added as below
1kg	(2lb)	parsnips, turnips or carrots
15g	($\frac{1}{2}$oz)	cream of tartar
		Good sherry yeast culture
		Pectic enzyme

Water to: 4.5 litres (1 gallon)

Method:

Peel bananas and chop root vegetables and boil both in 2 litres (three pints) of water for half an hour. Strain liquor over grape concentrate, tartaric acid and cream of tartar (stir until latter dissolves). When cool add gypsum and yeast nutrient with vigorous stirring, and adjust gravity of must with syrup and water until you have 4.5 litres (1 gallon) at a gravity of between 110 and 120 (about 1.35kg sugar and 1.5 litre water). Add yeast and pectic enzyme and endeavour to obtain a long cool fermentation lasting up to two months.

Rack carefully into a container large enough to ensure a good air space above the wine and plug container with cotton wool. Keep in a temperature of 13°-17°C (55°-65°F) undisturbed by any movement for at least one year. If a flor forms, tasting must be done by carefully cutting a small hole in the yeast skin.

SHERRY
(Oloroso type)
(by P. Duncan and B. Acton)

Ingredients:

900g	**(2lb)**	**bananas**
1.3kg	**(3lb)**	**peaches**
		Yeast nutrient
450g	**(1lb)**	**chopped raisins**
15g	**($\frac{1}{2}$oz)**	**tartaric acid**
		Sherry wine yeast culture
		Sugar syrup to be added as below (syrup made by boiling up 900g (2lb) sugar with 570ml (1 pint) water)).

Method:

Peel bananas and boil in 2.25 litres (four pints) of water for half an hour. Strain water, boiling, over raisins and peaches. Mix in tartaric acid and leave to cool for 12 hours. Add nutrient and a vigorously

fermenting yeast starter. Ferment on pulp for three days then strain off pulp into gallon jar pressing fruit lightly, and bring volume up to 4 litres (seven pints). Check gravity periodically and add 150ml (quarter pint) doses of sugar syrup every time the gravity falls to 5.

When fermentation is complete, rack very carefully and place in container larger than amount of wine, allowing good air space and plug with cotton wool plug only. Leave in a warm place (around 25°C (75°F)) for at least three months (or longer if temperature is cooler than this). A flor should not normally develop in this case but a good sherry flavour will result.

Sweeten to taste when bottling.

Both recipes are of course better if minimum quantity of three gallons is made.

SLOE WINE

Ingredients:

1.3kg	(3lb)	sloes
225g	($\frac{1}{2}$lb)	raisins
1.3kg	(3lb)	sugar
3.5 litres (6 pints)		water
		Yeast and nutrient

Method:

Much the same as for elderberry. Mash the sloes well, pour over them the boiling water, and then add the minced raisins and two pounds of sugar. Stir well, cool to 20°C (70°F), add yeast, cover with a cloth, and leave to ferment in a warm room for 10 days. Then strain on to remaining sugar and pour into fermenting jar. Thereafter, continue as for elderberry. If the wine towards the end of the fermentation is a little too bitter, as it may be, a little more sugar can be added, 100g (4oz) at a time. Usually such additions will be unnecessary. The remarks about colour loss and maturing time apply equally to sloe as to elderberry. A blend of two-thirds elderberry, one-third sloe is, I find, usually about right, if the above recipes are used, but each is an excellent wine in its own right.

TABLE WINE

(Red, Dry)

(by P. Duncan and B. Acton)

Ingredients:

5kg	**(12lb)**	**elderberries or 3½lb dried elderberries**
2.5kg	**(6lb)**	**raisins**
		Yeast nutrient
3.5kg	**(8lb)**	**sugar**
		acid (preferable ⅓ malic, ⅓ citric, ⅓ tartaric)
		mixture 4 level tablespoons
		Grey Owl Pommard Yeast

Water to: 20 litres (4½ gallons)

Method:

Crush elderberries and chop raisins and add 13.5 litres (3 gallons) cold water plus 3 Campden tablets. After 24 hours add yeast nutrient

". . .and now a few words about mead. . ."

and an actively fermenting yeast starter. Ferment on pulp for a further two days, stirring pulp into the must twice daily, then strain off the pulp and press lightly. Add all the sugar in the form of syrup and make up total quantity to 20 litres (4½ gallons) with water and add acid. Ferment to dryness and rack into a cask. Rack initially four months later and then as required by cask conditions. The wine should remain in cask for 15-18 months, after which it can be bottled and should remain in bottle for 12 months before consumption. It should by this time have acquired a pleasant character possibly reminiscent of a Burgundy, with an alcohol content of 12½% by volume.

TANGERINE WINE

Ingredients:

		12-15 tangerines
1.25kg	(2lb 11oz)	sugar
		Yeast and nutrient
Water to: 4.5 litres (1 gallon)		

Method:

Peel the tangerines and crush them by hand. Discard the peel. Pour 3.5 litres (6 pints) of boiling water over the crushed fruit, and leave it to soak for 12 hours. Strain, and warm the juice to assist the sugar to dissolve. Pour the juice over the sugar and stir until all the sugar is dissolved. Cool to 70°F and add the yeast (a wine yeast or a level teaspoon of granulated yeast). Pour into fermentation jar and fit trap. When ferment slows top up with cold water. Ferment until finished and the wine is clear; then rack into clean bottles. A lovely delicate wine.

TANSY WINE

(Tanacetum vulgare)

Ingredients:

		1 small packet Tansy Herb
1.3kg	(3lb)	parsnips
1.3kg	(3lb)	sugar
15g	(½oz)	citric acid (or 3 lemons, no pith, in lieu)
		A pinch of grape tannin
		Sufficient water to produce 4.5 litres (1 gallon) must
		Yeast nutrient and activated wine yeast

116

Method:

Clean by scrubbing the parsnips, then slice thinly and boil in 3 litres (5 pints 5oz) of water until just tender, but not mushy, otherwise the wine will not fall bright. Strain the liquid on to the sugar and stir until dissolved. Next pour 600ml (1 pint) of boiling water over the tansy herb and infuse as in making tea. When cool add the tansy infusion, citric acid and cold tea to the sweetened parsnip extract. Add the yeast nutrient and activated wine yeast and ferment under an air lock in the normal way. The tansy herb should be used sparingly as it is rather hot yet at the same time pleasant and aromatic, and is used often in lieu of ginger.

"If my wife knew I had as much as this, she'd have half the village down here, sampling. . ."

GREEN TOMATO WINE
(by C. Shave)

Ingredients:

1.3kg	(3lb)	green tomatoes
1 litre	(1 quart)	balm leaves including stalks
450g	(1lb)	raisins, sultanas or currants
450g	(1lb)	maize, barley or wheat
		2 lemons or oranges (or 15g ($\frac{1}{2}$oz citric acid))
1.3kg	(3lb)	sugar
		pinch of grape tannin
		activated yeast and nutrient

Water to: 4.5 litres (1 gallon)

Method:

Soak the grains overnight in a little extra water. Scald the dried fruit and pass the grains, leaves and stalks together with the tomatoes, dried fruit and fruit rinds (no white pith) through a mincer. Place the minced ingredients in the fermenting jar and add the sugar. Pour 3 litres (5lb 5oz) boiling water over this and stir well to dissolve the sugar. When cool add the cold tea, fruit juices or citric acid, activated yeast and nutrient. Ferment for seven days then strain into glass jar, topping up to bottom of neck with cold water. Fit air lock, ferment and rack in the normal way.·

WHEAT
(see Barley)

WHEAT AND ORANGE
(see under Orange and Wheat)

WHEAT AND PRUNE
(see under Prune)

YARROW WINE
(Achillea-Millefolium)

Also known as Milfoil, the Yarrow is a weed found in pastures, roadside wastes, and on commons. In winemaking the flowers and bruised leaves (no stalk) are used. The yarrow flowers from June to the end of the year.

Ingredients:

4 litres	(1 gallon)	yarrow flowers and bruised leaves
450g	(1lb)	chopped raisins
1kg	(2.2lb)	sugar
		a pinch of grape tannin
		2 oranges
		2 lemons (or 15g ($\frac{1}{2}$oz) citric acid)
		activated yeast and nutrient

Water to: 4.5 litres (1 gallon)

Method:

Remove the blooms and put them into a bowl with the chopped raisins; pour 3.5 litres (6 pints) of boiling water over them, and leave to soak for four or five days, then strain into a pan and add the thinly peeled skins of the oranges (no white pith) and the sugar, and simmer for 20 minutes. Add the juice of the oranges and lemons (or citric acid) and the tea; stir, then strain immediately into a bowl or polythene bucket and allow to cool to 20°C (70°F). Add yeast and nutrient, keep well covered in a warm place for 7 days, until the first vigorous ferment has died down, then transfer to a fermenting jar and fit a fermentation lock. Top up to bottom of neck with cold water if necessary. Wait until all fermentation has ceased – usually about two months – then rack for the first time. A second racking two or three months later will be beneficial if a second yeast deposit forms, and this time your yarrow wine can be bottled. Keep it at least six months before you drink it.

INDEX

Acid 7
Almond (Calcavella) 9
Ammonium Phosphate 6
Ammonium Sulphate 6
Apple 9
Apricot and Date (*see* Date and Apricot) 55
Apricot Sherry 11

Bakers' Brewers' Yeast 6
Banana 11
Spiced 13
Dried 13
and Dried Elderberry 14
— Fig 15
— Parsnip 15
— Prune 16
— Rice 16
— Rosehip Shell 18
Dried, and Rosehip 18
and Sarsaparilla 19
Barley 20
Beers and Stouts 21
Berrybrew 22
Boys' Bitter 23
Morgan's Ale 21
Oatmeal Stout 24
Seward's Ale 25
Beetroot 27
and Parsnip 27
— Pineapple 28
Bilberry 52
Dried 57
Blackberry (1) 29
(2) 30
Blackcurrant 30
Bottling 7
Broom 31
Bullace 32

Cabbage 34
Campden Tablets 5
Carbon Dioxide 5
Carnation 36
Carrot 37
Carum Carvi (Caraway Seed and Tea) 34
Carvi Fructus (Caraway Seed and Wheat) 36
Chamomile 38
Chempro 5
Cherry (1) 39
(2) 40
Plum 92
Christmas Drinks 41
Ale Punch 44

Che-na-grum 42
Old-time Punch 41
Spiced Cider Comforter 42
Wassail Bowl 43
Wine Cup 42
Clary 44
Cleaning Solutions 5
Cleanliness 5
Coffee 46
Coltsfoot, Broom 32
Concentrates (Fruit Juice) 47
Cider or Perry 47
Cyser 48
Heavy Sweet Apple or Pear 48
Light Apple or Pear 48
Rhubarb and Apple 48
Crab Apple (1) 48
— (2) 49
Currant 50
and Raisin 50
Black 30
Red (1) 98
Red (2) 99

Damson 51
Dandelion 52
Date 54
— and Apricot 55
Dos and Don'ts 8

Elderberry Wines, with Variations 56
1. Ecstatic Elderberry 56
2. Elderberry Enchant 58
3. Non pareil 58
4. Ambrosia 58
5. Créme de Raisin 59
6. Vino Magnifico 59
7. Elderberry and Apple 60
8. As You Like it 60
9. Aromatic Splendour 60
10. Herbal Nectar 60
11. Dried 61
Elderberry (Dried) and Banana 14
Elecampane 62
Equipment 4
Extraction 7

Fennel 62
Fermentation 7
Fig 64
Fig and Banana (*see* Banana) 15
— Parsnip (*see* Parsnip and Fig) 88
— Sultana 64
Fruit Juices (*see* Concentrates) 47

121

INDEX

Ginger 66
  Glow 66
Goat's-Beard 67
Golden Rod 68
Grape and Sultana 68
Greengage 70

Hawthornberry 70
Herbal Delight 72
Huckleberry 72
Hypochlorite 5

Introducing this Book 3

Juice Extractor 5

Kohl Rabi 73

Lavender 74
Legal Position 4
Limeflower 74
Loganberry 75

Madeira-type 76
Maize (*see* Barley) 20
Malmsey-type 78
Mint 78
Mulberry 79

Nutrient 6

Oakbud 80
Oakleaf 80
Onion 82
Orange and Wheat 82
Oxalic Acid 100
Seville Orange 83
Sweet Orange 84

Parsley and Rice 84
Parsnip 86
Parsnip Wine Spiced 86
  and Banana (*see* Banana) 15
  — Beetroot 27
  — Fig 88
Peach Perfection 89
Pectinol 5
Pektolase 5
Pineapple and Beet (*see* Beet and
    Pineapple) 28

Plum (1) 91
  (2) 92
  (Cherry) 92
Port-type 94
Pressing 7
Protection 7
Prune 95
  and Banana 16
  — Wheat 96
Pumpkin 97

Racking 7
Red Currant (1) 98
  (2) 99
Rhubarb, with Variations 100
  1. Golden Dream 100
  2. Memorable Nectar 101
  3. Golden Pipkin 102
  4. Christmas Port 102
  5. Winter Cheer 102
Rice 20, 103
  (Chinese) 104
  (English Version) 106
  and Banana (*see* under Banana) 16
  and Parsley (*see* under Parsley) 84
Rohament P, 5
Rosehip 106
  (Dried) 107
  Shell and Fig 108
  and Dried Banana 18
  Syrup 109
Rosemary 110

Sarsaparilla and Banana 19
Sauternes 111
Sherry (Dry Fino) 112
  (Oloroso) 113
Sloe 114
Soda 5
Sterilising Solution 5
Sugar 5

Table, Red, Dry 115
Tangerine 116
Tannin 7
Tansy 116
Tomato, Green 118

Utensils 4

Vitamin B1 6

INDEX

Welcome to Winemaking 4
What Wine is 5
Wheat (*see* Barley) 20
Wheat and Orange (*see* Orange and
    Wheat) 82
— Prune (*see* under Prune) 96
Winemaking Summarised 7

Yarrow 119
Yeast 6

MAKING WINES LIKE THOSE YOU BUY
Bryan Acton & Peter Duncan

Making Wines Like Those you Buy tells you how to make at home, cheaply and from easily available ingredients, white, red and rosé table wines, Sauternes, Hocks, Moselles, Madeiras and champagne plus a wide variety of liqueurs and aperitifs.

FIRST STEPS IN WINEMAKING
C. J. J. Berry

Universally known as 'the Winemaker's Bible', this book is an inspiration to beginners in winemaking. It covers terminology, basic facts and techniques and also gives an invaluable month by month guide to seasonal recipes for wine. Wines from fruit, flowers, vegetables, foliage, dried fruit and wine kits, showing wine and judging – you will find it all in this book.

HOME BREWED BEERS AND STOUTS
C. J. J. Berry

The first modern book on home brewing, this was an instant success when it was first published in 1963. This latest edition contains up-to-date information on how to brew fine beers and stouts of authentic flavour and strength for as little as 6p a pint!